BOARDWALK REPUBLIC

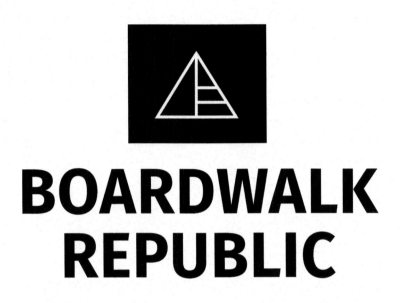

BOARDWALK
REPUBLIC

Miles Shades

NEW DEGREE PRESS

COPYRIGHT © 2021 MILES SHADES

All rights reserved.

BOARDWALK REPUBLIC

ISBN

978-1-63730-341-2 *Paperback*

978-1-63730-342-9 *Kindle Ebook*

978-1-63730-343-6 *Digital Ebook*

To the international seafarers who were stranded aboard
multinational cruise ships during the COVID-19 pandemic, many
of whom lost their lives or livelihoods upon repatriation.

To the constituents of Atlantic City and the
Greater South Jersey community, (NJ-2).

To Holland America Cruise Line for serving as a
vessel for cultural diplomacy worldwide.

To Georgetown University for continuing to mentor students
as they become men and women in the service of others.

To the people of the United States of America and the United
Kingdom, for fostering mutual understanding and global citizenship.

CONTENTS

—

Imagine a world untethered from the docks of tradition.
Wading into an ocean of possibilities,
floating peacefully with the tide.
Imagine a world that surrenders to its currents.
Drifting across borders until neither can exist while the
other persists, a nautical paradox waiting to be resolved.
Or absolved from its role in a bigger production.
One choreographed to enlighten, to broaden, to unite...
A world fractured by consumption, sickened by
possession, castaway by a generation of neglect.
Imagine a company that can show
the world of the world...
A vessel of diplomacy to trump an era
of lust, of exploitation, of greed.
Imagine an experience that transcends the need to
create, to debate, or even fabricate the façade of connection
rooted in every port of call. In every interaction or reaction
of the people and places encountered in our wake.
Imagine a company that can show
the world of the world...
Would you join?
Or would you subside?
You've been chosen to chart a new course. For
wonder or plight, adventure or tragedy.
Will you embark on a voyage less traveled?
That blurs the edge of place and time,
where countries become constrictions
to divide yours from mine.

—MILES SHADES

AUTHOR'S NOTE

Imagine the possibility of pledging allegiance aboard a floating city, endlessly sailing toward ports-of-call across every region of the world. What would you choose to explore in the Alaskan wilderness? Who would you venture to meet in the markets of Africa? How would you reconcile the promise of adventure with the comforts of tradition?

Over the past four years, I've spent months at sea with a team of international seafarers. The routine of waking up in a new destination, exploring the local surroundings, and returning to share our adventures with thousands of passengers became a daily enrichment experience. One that more people all over the world *should* have the opportunity to explore.

The longer we floated aboard this international city, the harder it was to envision a traditional life on land. Unshackled from the confines of a cubicle, an overwhelming sense of purpose fundamentally changed our traditional outlooks on the world.

Travel gives perspective to our lives as a sequence of experiences, rather than an object—fatal to ignorance, nationalism, greed, and possession. The more we engage with foreign lands and encounter the real people who inhabit them, the stronger our sense of empathy becomes. We begin to define ourselves not only as residents of our local communities and home countries but as citizens of a larger world.

The cruise industry has recently been torpedoed. Decimated by a once-in-a-century pandemic, marooning thousands of seafaring passengers and crew.

What will this form of travel become as we embrace the mobile mind-shift of a post-pandemic world? How can we balance the thirst for travel with the integrity of our environment? The current perception of the industry defines this experience as merely a vacation, a relaxing opportunity to unwind, recharge, and passively explore popular destinations through the comfort of a cabin porthole.

That is, until now.

Imagine the thrill of a relentless expedition, spanning the seven seas across every region of the world!

Historically, most cruise passengers are between the ages of 40-75. Don't wait to broaden your horizons.

What are the true cultural effects of empowering younger generations to charter this voyage in their formative years as global citizens?

Boardwalk Republic explores the uncharted potential of a life at sea. Exploring broader themes of adventure vs. tradition, possession vs. experience, and responsible tourism. All of this is encompassed within a time of rebirth for both the cruise industry and Atlantic City, NJ, USA.

You will take this journey with Max, a disillusioned boy who ventures away from his hometown, searching for something more. Tempted by the traditional vices of greed and lust for possession, Max clashes with his rival, Price, as he struggles to take control of the helm of *M.S. World One.* Our budding adventurer must chart a new course for his generation to reconcile the lessons from the past with the hope of progress in the future.

Whatever your ambition, from wherever in our world you hail, let this journey broaden your horizons... if you're courageous enough to set sail.

Welcome aboard,

Miles "Shades" Schoedler

AN EMPIRE OF SANDCASTLES

———

The vanishing prints of a runner's stride faded within wind-swept sand beneath the deep rhythmic breath of the coastal breeze. He strode past fallen resorts, defamed hotels, and steel doors that preserved the shells of summers past. A battered sign remembered a distant echo, reading: *One Atlantic Ocean.*

A boardwalk married the coast. Built for parades of prominence, the weathered wood now cracked under an approaching thunder of footsteps. Clouds converged, casting ominous shadows on abandoned marquis, while rain washed away the sorrow of an era bankrupt of virtue and bliss.

Upon reaching the end, the man paused for a moment. Resting, he borrowed a shell from the barren dunes and signed his name on the back—*Max.*

Better suited here than on the side of a decaying building. He flicked it back into the surf for another chance to become sand. Rejecting his sentiment, the tide retrieved the shell, floating it back beneath his feet as it crashed into the remnants of a board game. Plastic pieces, thimbles, and counterfeit bills littered the shore.

What kind of a town breeds a game like this? He tossed the rulebook aside.

Block after block was lined with strip clubs, crippled storefronts, broken windows, and flashing signs proudly displaying the name of whichever casino owner laid claim to that plot of land the summer before. *Feels like the only strategy keeping this town afloat each year is a reoccurring Get out of Jail Free Card.* He stretched beneath the entrance of a boardwalk hotel gleaming like a lighthouse across the Absecon Inlet.

Staggering into the lobby, he clipped a glass bottle poised atop a worn counter. It fell to the floor, shattering into pieces that echoed throughout the empty reception, revealing a message: *Atlantic City, the world's long-lost Port-of-Call.*

Port-of-Call? Where have I seen this phrase before...?

Premonitions of cargo voyages, expeditions, shipwrecks, and conquistadors flooded his imagination like a thick fog. He fantasized shaking hands with Columbus, Magellan, Cook, and Crusoe.

Intrigued, he walked through the hotel, mesmerized by paintings of storms at sea and nautical charts. What a life this could be... He imagined tinkering with rusty sextants and telescopes as he climbed to the rooftop terrace.

Overlooking the skyline, he cringed at the blatant overdevelopment and cultural decadence polluting the streets below. Trucks hauled nothing but empty space as they squeezed through crowded alleyways, beeping at idle sports cars and sluggish pedestrians in narrow crosswalks. Shoppers fumbled with overflowing bags of plastic objects in a never-ending frenzy of buy and sell.

Max sighed, disgusted by it all. *Is this all there is to life? Work your whole career for scraps just so you can afford to buy useless junk?*

Winter hung over Atlantic City like a noose. It always had. The cold time here was quiet as a graveyard. For six months, you could have it all to yourself because the first hint of winter's arrival always sent the tourists scattering like hotel roaches, and they didn't return until the weather was hot enough to sizzle their pasty skin.

That was precisely why Max liked the winter. It provided him a vacation from the vacationers.

It wasn't so much the crowds that bothered him. It was the type that made him uneasy. The locals called them the 'shoobies,' and they were too... polished. Vacation was treated like a job to them. It was too important to be anything other than perfect. They were a completely different breed than the present company of the winter crowd, which consisted of mostly elderly gambling addicts, the off-season thrift vacationers, and quasi-suicidal loners who preferred the streets void of any life. To Max, the winter crowd were a refreshing bunch of people compared to the snowbirds who flocked there in summer.

Max idolized the emptiness of the boardwalk in winter. It stood broad, open, and proud against the continuous crashing of icy Atlantic waves. At the end of its pier, despite the threat of bristling wind and waves with cruel intentions, he could often clear his head. Today he needed that. The wind wasn't forbidding visitors today like usual. It was needle-point cold, but he would brave it. A walk to the end of the pier and back was just what he needed. To think, walk, and be alone.

Max looked out over the ocean from the end of the boardwalk. Beyond its horizon, out somewhere farther than what he could see. His vision was directed inward, where his thoughts battered and bounced off his skull like a moth caught in a lampshade. "What am I going to do now?" he muttered to the waves, as if they were suspect for his displeasure. "What the hell am I going to do?"

A contemptuous frown curled over his upper lip. His fingers flexed and opened, not to warm themselves from the biting cold but because of stress fueled by his anger. It felt like the weight of the earth was piling up between his eyes, and as if his jaw had snapped shut like an iron-tooth bear trap. He was glad to be alone. He let out a scream that rattled his own innards.

Only the waves heard Max, but they weren't interested. They just continued rolling toward him, intent as ever to break themselves on whatever stood in their way. The spray shot upward like a rocket, with enough water squeezing through the planking of the boardwalk to drench his weary soul. "Goddamn ocean! You did this on purpose!"

The wind's light chill was now suddenly amplified by the wet fabric of his freshly baptized body. He wanted to hurry off the damn boardwalk. Half limping, half jogging, he made it to the looming steps of the Ocean Resort and hailed a cab downtown.

The city was a checkerboard of dive bars and upscale restaurants. Like most iconic cities along the northeast coast, A.C. had struggled tremendously to survive. Now, the city was growing. Its rising popularity was most evident in the neighborhoods clinging to the city center. They were transforming from rundown, regular places, to chic upscale joints hoping to snag hipsters, yuppies, and whoever else wanted to overpay for a dwelling. The seasons were no longer keeping out the vacationers. It looked like Atlantic City was finally hoping they would stay.

Where can a guy get a drink around here this time of year? He slammed the cab door shut as he staggered into the old Ritz Carlton hotel lobby.

Hobbling up the stairwell, he shouldered open the door to an ancient marble ballroom. Just as expected, there were only a handful of patrons in the bar. All of them were drinking alone, seated close to the wall or a corner so as to be left that way. Max copied their lead and found himself a seat at the edge of the bar. Above him, the TV displayed the results of the latest off-track betting.

The barman nodded at Max's gesture for a pint, filled a glass, and then plopped it down on a warped coaster, leaving him to drink and drift off into his thoughts like all good afternoon bar customers.

One pint turned into three before Max noticed the sun had already disappeared. It was still early, but now the shadow of Atlantic City's newest addition to the skyline eclipsed the low-hanging winter sun. The Price Family's latest monstrosity, The Ivory Tower, cast its thirty-six-story shadow over the bar's entire block, a bleak foreshadowing of things to come. Soon this bar would be demolished, its memories eradicated and replaced by the stain-resistant carpet of some new five-star casino.

Max made an internal effort to enjoy it while it lasted. Before it turned into something… inauthentic.

He was just starting to enjoy the depressing weight of the bar's atmosphere when the front door flung open with a bang.

"Not again," the barman muttered and rolled his eyes. Though clearly annoyed by this new arrival, the barman didn't protest. Instead, he reached for the tip-top of the bottle shelf behind the bar. Forcing a smile, he greeted the regular, "Good to see you again, Mr. Martin. Here you go," he added while topping off a couple of strong pours of gin.

"That's my boy, Curtis!" the new patron bellowed. "Be a king and give everyone in the bar a shot of it!"

Max sighed. He didn't want to share this melancholic, quiet space with a hotshot. Not after today. He'd met his daily quota of ego clashes. Especially now. Especially from this guy.

Max studied the obnoxious man out of the corner of his eye through a mirror behind the bar. He was shorter, though solidly built like his lifetime had been spent in manual labor, or at least that's how he wanted to be perceived.

Finally turning his head to look the man in the eye, Max noticed it was a glass eye. Hidden behind a monocle. He was even more brutish up close. A flat, wide nose that had clearly been broken many times spanned his face. His eyes were set close. His skin was yellowed with age and drooping from smoke, and his head was covered carelessly by a black top hat.

Max, like most people, wasn't a fan of arrogance. He tried to ignore the man and looked straight ahead at the bar. But his mind was swimming with questions about this total stranger. *What gives him the right to act like that? Where did he get the money to buy a bunch of afternoon patrons shots during the offseason?*

As if he somehow heard Max's thoughts, the loudmouth approached him, striking his cane to the floor with each stride like a battle drum. He sat down on the barstool next to Max and stared at his profile through the glass for a moment with a sidelong smirk. "Whatcha drinkin', kid?" he asked with a thick New Yorker accent, glaring ahead into his reflection behind the bottles.

Though he desperately wanted to, Max didn't have the guts to ignore a direct question. "Beer," he mumbled. "Just having a beer."

Martin motioned to the bartender, who was still pouring the shots. "Bring them shots over here with a beer, would ya?" With that, he plunked down a wad of cash. The bills were wrinkled and oddly folded as if it wasn't money in his pockets but receipts. From the mishmash, he pulled out three hundred-dollar bills, all multicolored and embroidered with a bold letter 'M'.

"That oughta cover it, no? You keep the change on this one. Get yourself somethin' special."

The bartender nodded slowly and kept pouring.

"So, what's your name, kid?" Martin pried.

"It's Max."

"Max what?" Martin asked again, somewhat rhetorically as he checked his watch.

"Max Shades."

Martin rolled back his chair, tapping his cane on the bar. "Is that your real name or you pullin' my leg?"

"Yup. That's my real name," Max said with a dismissive sigh. He wanted to be left alone, but it wasn't working.

"So, what brings a smart-looking guy like you into a place like this?" Martin pressed, fidgeting restlessly in his seat.

"I was in town for a job interview. It didn't go as well as I'd hoped." Max's voice cracked as he tried to conceal his anguish.

"I'm sorry to hear that, kid. What was it for? Banking or something?"

"No, not really. Kind of. It was a good job with an online real estate development group. I really thought I was gonna get it."

"A what?" Martin smirked.

"A real estate agency, but online. It was with the company that made the new Jolly Roger app for demand forecasting." Max caught himself clipping his words with a tinge of frustration. He didn't want to explain the basics of e-commerce to an old man.

"Jolly Roger, huh? Can't say that I heard of it," Martin replied with no sense of Max's intolerance. "Musta been a big deal if it's got you so blue."

"It was," Max replied, shaking his head. "If I had gotten that job, then it would've been smooth sailing. The salary was three times what I make now."

"Well, that's too bad." Martin faked his sincerity.

The barman finally arrived with their drinks. He palmed the $300 without so much as a thank you. The ungrateful attitude did nothing to sour Martin's spirits. He was gleaming at the look of his frothy beer. He elbowed Max and said, "Look at this, kid. Ain't she a beauty? Cheers!"

They guzzled down nearly the entire pint.

Martin continued, slurring his words, "I came to Atlantic City because the mayor is naming a board game after me.

Something about acquiring land, trading properties, securing a comfortable little portfolio for retirement, charging rents for players to stay in my buildings. Ever heard of it?"

Max gripped the bottom of his glass with an iron fist, imagining the sense of relief that smashing it into the TV screens behind the bar would bring. Their radiant static still broadcasting the latest slot machine odds. *Have I ever heard of that game? Who hasn't? This guy really can't see beyond the mirage of his monocle.*

"Sounds like you're building an Empire." Max steadied his temper, checking his watch and racking his brain for an excuse to leave.

Oblivious to his discontent, Martin continued, "When I was a kid, it was the only game we played as a family." He stretched his cane behind the stool, cracking his back as he inhaled a deep breath. "We played it every time we went on summer vacation. I loved that game. I was good at it, but I was always tryin' to figure out how I could beat my brother. So, one day I finally figured out the best way to play my hand and get just what I wanted. I was like the little king of real estate! I loved it! Anyway, I came here to see how Atlantic City changed, because I was put in prison for bankrupting the city thirty years ago."

Max slid his stool back away from the bar, distancing himself in a panic with the realization that he was now min- gling with an ex-con.

Martin continued, "When I finally got out and recouped my money, I wanted to come here to spend it. Pretend like I was buying Boardwalk or something. I mean, I didn't know where else to go, so I just came here. Turns out not much has changed since I was locked up. It still sucks here in the winter."

Max chuckled a shallow laugh, giving Martin one last chance for redemption. "Yeah, it does sometimes. But sometimes it's okay. I like it better here in winter than summer myself." he replied, scanning the bar for a sense of comfort and eyeing the exits.

"Yeah, I could tell."

"How could you tell?"

"Well, when I first saw you, you reminded me of me. I'm more of a winter guy, so I guess I just figured you are, too."

Max didn't like the comparison. "Oh, I don't usually drink in the daytime. I'm just having a rough day is all."

"No, I don't mean the drinking. I mean the way you were sitting there staring off into nothing. Lost in the visions of your imagination."

Max didn't get it, and he didn't like what the man was implying. He'd certainly seen more than just the inside of a jail cell in the last two decades.

"Kid, I know the difference between having a bad day and feeling bad. You are the feeling bad type I think."

"I don't agree." Max had enough and finally rose to leave.

"I know. I know, I'll get to the point." Martin rolled up his sleeves and gave Max his monocle, gesturing for him to peer through it at the mirror behind the bar in front of them.

"I thought about seein' the world. Being caged for that long, I wanted to make up for lost time, ya know? So, I bought a cruise because my dad went on one when I was a kid, and he always talked about it as a fun thing to do when I was growing up, so I bought this one leaving out of Atlantic City."

"Well, then what are you waiting for? Why are you wasting your time up here with me?" Max barked, losing patience.

"It's not that simple, kid. You see... people round here found out I was back in town. And apparently, they're still upset that I robbed the *Community Chest* and never paid them for building my resorts. So, they served me another court order. Community Service, *for life*."

"You robbed your own people? Martin... why?" Max shoved him off his bar stool, causing a scene. "Who are you? Don't lie to me! *Who are you!*"

"Price... Martin Price." The old man tried to collect himself, leaning on his cane for support as he clambered up off the floor.

"As in the Price Family? The owner of Price Plaza? The casino built on the blood, sweat, and tears of your fellow citizens... who you swindled for their life savings!?"

Realizing he'd revealed too much, Martin said defensively, "Well, as you can tell, people are still upset about it."

"How do you sleep at night?" Max reprimanded.

"Okay, okay, okay, kid. There's still a lot you don't know. You only have one side of the story. But no matter. It's too late for me now anyway. But I'd like to make up for it. Somehow..." Martin patted his pockets, searching for the ticket. "I want you to take the cruise instead."

The barman had wandered closer to address the scuffle and been caught eavesdropping. "You've been doing nothing but talking about that damn cruise all week," he interjected, waving a bottle-opener like a heavy finger poised to discipline. "I've had to hear about it for hours every day, and now you're just going to give it to this guy? If you're gonna give it to anyone, it should be me for putting up with hearing about it. *Get out!* Both of you!"

Afternoon cusped into dusk as they hobbled down the stairwell and dodged sour looks from hotel guests on their walk of shame toward the exit. Slipping through the revolving doors and out onto the boardwalk, Martin leaned against a graffitied wall to pull a cigarette from his jacket. He lit one for Max, who politely refused.

"Listen, kid. Here's the deal." Martin took a ticket from his pocket and unfolded it from the rest of the branded bills lining the inseam. "Take this cruise. You'll never get this opportunity again."

Max reached out his hand to reluctantly accept it.

"You have to be at the pier this evening," Martin explained as he lay the ticket in his hand.

"You mean tonight? I won't have time to pack."

"It's a special all-inclusive boat. They told me specifically not to pack. I'm sure it's the same for you."

"So, I just show up and they let me onboard with your ticket?"

"Yeah, that's exactly it."

"When they check my ID, they won't let me onboard."

"I'm sure they will, actually."

"Why would they do that?"

"Look at the ticket."

Max looked down. Inscribed in gold leaf cursive across a paper thicker than a wedding invitation, was his name: *Max Shades. The bearer of this ticket shall be granted passage aboard MS. World One.*

"How did you do that?" Max asked with his eyes still engrossed by the intricacy of the ticket. "How the hell did you do that?" He flipped it over, revealing a branded globe separating the name of the ship in three-dimensional mystique.

Awestruck, he glanced back up for a sense of clarity, only to find himself staring at his reflection in the glass panels of the historic hotel. The silhouette of the old man tipped his hat and vanished, swept away like sand in the winter winds.

A LABYRINTH
OF LANTERNS

———

Atlantic City—where dreams come to die. The sun was low and sinking fast. What was left of its light was long, icepick-thin slants that still managed to squeeze through the rows of hotels and condos. Before long, the ocean would be no more than a sound somewhere in the eastern blackness. Max made his way in that direction, hoping to reach the pier in time. After a series of crosswalks and some jaywalking, he was back at the boardwalk. The wind there had become agitated and raw. It flung shards of sand into Max's eyes. He squinted, gritting his teeth and turning his shoulder into the frigid blast. The ticket flopped and swished in his hand as if the wind were trying to snatch it.

Playground Pier was the latest installment in the city's tourism expansion project. It was meant to catapult the number of new visitors by a hundred thousand in the first year of operation. But just as it proudly announced it was open and ready for business, the city hiked its luxury taxes and mooring fees. The ships wouldn't be steaming their engines any time soon. A city that based its economy on selling luck now found itself woefully unlucky. Instead of a stream of tourists flooding the rod iron gates of the entrance, they were tightly chained shut. Above the gates was an archway proclaiming *Welcome to the World's Playground*. Not a soul had passed underneath its welcoming words.

"You gotta be kidding me," Max lamented at being locked out as he pulled hopelessly at the gate's thick iron bars.

The place was deserted. The wind's biting cold that afternoon was enough to dishearten even the sturdiest of afternoon walkers. The boardwalk was a ghost town, even for January. Shadows edged closer as Max looked from one abandoned end to another.

He breathed a sigh of relief. What followed was confusion. Maybe he had the wrong place? He turned his back to the wind and unfolded the ticket. To his amazement, it no longer spelled out his name in shining gold calligraphy but instead the passage read:

The gates to beyond only open when pushed
And chains only fall when they're pulled
Locks will spring open if asked
For they always do as they're told.

Max's brow furrowed. This couldn't be his ticket. He patted and reached into the other pockets of his jacket and upturned the lining from his pants pockets, exposing their empty seams like rabbit ears. He had no other possessions other than his wallet and phone. This was his ticket, somehow cryptically instructing him like a mystic shadow. Max looked around again. This time for a hidden camera that was certainly recording every minute reaction of his bewilderment. He was too embarrassed of being the butt of a joke to do as the poem instructed, but a visceral curiosity got the better of him.

Reluctantly, he lifted his hand. "Hey, there, Lock," he said sheepishly. "This is Max. I'm supposed to catch a ship here today, so I was wondering if you could open for me."

Softly, he tugged at the lock. Its U-bolt sprung quickly as the spring of mouse trap. "Ahh!" Max burst with surprise. He then gave a quick, downward tug. The chain unfurled and clanged on the pavement at his feet.

Awestruck, Max looked again at the poem. With a slight push of his palm, the towering, imposing gates yielded. They slowly opened, moaning in protest on hinges unaccustomed to swinging. Playground Pier lay fully open before him. Max tucked the ticket into his jacket pocket and stepped forward.

Twilight shifted into a heavy gray, mixed with a fog that had rolled in from somewhere beyond the horizon. Together they had swallowed up both the ocean and the city and made Max feel marooned between the known and unknown, between day and night. Like a pilgrim who had taken his first steps toward Jerusalem, Max was leaving behind the past and any certainty for the future. He looked at his watch in disdain. He'd already walked back and forth twice to confirm he was in the right spot.

"This *is* Playground Pier," he muttered to the empty chamber.

Suddenly, a foghorn blasted somewhere in the distance. Max perked up to look, with a well of nerves throbbing in his gut. He hoped it was the ship, then he hoped that it wasn't. He was stretched between the thrill of pending adventure and frightening abandonment of the familiar.

He scanned what he could see of the waves, expecting to see the outline of a ship steaming toward him. After what felt like an eternity came and went, he watched, and then waited. Still, there was nothing. Not even a dinghy.

He turned on his heels to face reality when a lonesome gull cried out from the void, struggling to squawk over the sound of breaking waves crashing into the pier.

He squinted into the fog, where he could barely make out the right angles of a structure. Were it not for the floodlights dimmed and haloed by the mist, he'd not have seen it at all. Nothing stirred around it, and there was no way a camera's lens could cut through the fog, especially not at twilight. Still, he had to be sure. He walked as if in slow motion toward the building. With each step a small portion of it would sharpen until he was up close enough to take in the view of it without feeling as though he had scales over his eyes. There was no one there and nothing that looked like a hidden camera. He was alone.

Thoroughly disgusted at his naïveté, he headed toward the glass doors of the terminal building. Staying at this point would be insulting even to his intelligence.

"There's no ship. This isn't a magic ticket," he said as he felt the heavy weight of anger burden each pace toward the exit. He reached for the door handle; his mood now fully lathered into a justified rage. "Goddammit! What the hell is going on?"

He banged his head on a heavy iron object hanging from the exit doors. Its caged frame protected the subtle luminescence of an Edison bulb, somewhat suspended in the air like a mystical gas lantern.

He hoisted it from the wall and turned it back around, projecting its light farther and farther into the terminal as it revealed hidden fixtures and paranormal green direction lights along the baseboard. Following their path through a labyrinth of wooden boards enclosed from the winter gusts, he finally approached a lookout point with a pair of mounted binoculars. Anchored to the floor, their stone-cold viewfinders stared back at him like the gaze of a temptress, beaconing him in for a closer look.

Laying the lantern on the railing beside his perch, he peered through their lenses across the black horizon line of the sea for what felt like an eternity. Panning left and right, left and right, he scanned the scene until finally, he saw it. Row after row of lights were rising up from out of the blackness. They were sharp and clear, despite the wall of fog that separated them. As he focused their gaze to face whatever was surfacing, he was suddenly blinded. A flood of hard white light scorched into his eyes, forcing him to eject from the viewfinder and raise a forearm as a shield. Standing firm, he hoisted the mystic gas-lantern once again and strained to see the source of intrusion.

"Max Shades!" a voice boomed from behind the glare.

"Who's there?" Max stammered. "What do you want from me?" He swung the lantern back and forth as if warning the Americans of a pending British advance. *I thought it was two lanterns by sea, one if by land?*

"This is the *MS World One*. We are speaking to you from the bridge. Please don't be frightened!"

"I'm not frightened," Max quivered.

Above the booming voice behind the lights, a harsh blare of feedback pierced Max's ears. Then, a flurry of snickering followed by a muffled exchange. After that, a different voice took command of the light. One much richer, thickened with age and cigars. Max couldn't place the accent, though it was somewhere in Europe. "Max Shades, please forgive my bridge officers for their warped sense of humor. This is Lex Von Janssen, Captain of *M.S. World One*. We have arrived to grant you passage aboard our vessel."

"I can't see anything," Max shouted. "Can you please turn off the lights?"

"Of course, of course. Our apologies. Henk!" the captain yelled. "Off with the forward spotlight."

The sudden blackness left Max seeing a solar system of spots.

Before him, in an unparalleled glory, was the ship. It had risen like a submarine alongside the pier. In twilight's last moments, the full glory of its polished hull wasn't visible. It disappeared into the fog at both bow and stern, the stern side facing Max like a glorious iron wall. The smoke stacks, emblazoned with a flaming symbol, stretched beyond view into a darkening sky. Even from his ant-like view of the ship, there was no mistaking its splendor. This was a vessel constructed for no greater purpose than to explore and entertain in style.

Max was growing dizzy trying to determine its size. When he lowered his eyes, a set of flaming gas lanterns framed a doorway. It was the gangway, beckoning him like a portal to the unknown.

"Please proceed, Mr. Shades. We have a schedule to keep," the captain boomed from the fog above.

"You're twenty minutes late!" Max said wryly.

"I wasn't talking about your schedule," the captain retorted.

Max hesitated. "This is it." he whispered. "There is no going back."

Three hours ago, he was wallowing in self-pity. Everything he thought he'd ever wanted had slipped through his fingers. His life, as he'd planned it, had unraveled before it even began. What the old man had said was true. He didn't have a job or a girl. He didn't have purpose or aim, either. And he'd never had an adventure. There was a lot Max didn't have. At the moment, that included nothing to lose.

His leg moved almost by instinct, and he stepped forward, and again, each step effortless until he reached the end of the pier. Between him and the gangway stood ten feet of angry, churning, winter waves. Ten impossible feet separated him from the door. Certain death was below him with one missed step.

"We're waiting, Mr. Shades," the captain said with a tinge of irritation in his voice.

"Are you sure about this?" Max stammered. "This is how I'm supposed to board?" He waved his lantern over the deathly wake of the winter swells.

"Yes, Max. Now, please hurry. All aboard was twenty minutes ago, and like I said, we're in a bit of a hurry." the captain stressed.

Max couldn't see it, but it had to be there. It was too far to jump, so there had to be an invisible gangway connecting the pier to the ship. He told himself he couldn't see it because it was magical, just like the ticket and the ship itself. It was simply another test of his fortitude. Still, this seemed beyond rational. No one really ever stepped out in blind faith, at least outside the veil of fantasy films. *Especially* when stepping out meant falling to certain death.

His nerves were a herd of broncos, but he was determined to rein them in. His left foot hovered over the edge. The spray from a slapping wave against the concrete soaked his body anew. "I can do this. I can do this."

"Max! Wait!" the voice boomed over the loudspeaker. "There's no gangway there!"

"What? Why would you tell me to board?"

"Heavens, no! We would get sued for doing something like that! Henk!" the captain yelled away from the speaker's mouthpiece. "I said to put out the gangway this time!"

Max cried, "I can't do this!"

The gangway appeared from nothing. A ribbon of majestic red carpet, trimmed with gold thread, spread itself across the open space. Max tapped at it with his toe. It was solid as a mountain.

"Time is ticking, my son. It's time." the captain said.

A VOYAGE LESS TRAVELED

———

Meet me where our days begin and end, over the line where time stops ticking. A ghostly voice echoed through Max's head. Before he could second guess it, he bolted across the plush velvet inside the ship. Just inside the hull's archway, a pocket-watch flashed a bright blue hue as it lay fixed on a glass podium in an intricate atrium. Lined with artifacts from antiquity, the ornate marble rotunda preserved lessons from history as Max wandered closer to the watch. As he removed it, the podium retracted, revealing a hidden message inscribed in the floor below:

> *For those who seek and yet been found, your*
> *mission is simple and sure to renown...*
> *Embark on a voyage less traveled, blur the edge of*
> *place and time.*
> *Where countries become constrictions, to divide*
> *yours from mine.*

Suddenly, the floor opened. Emerging from the pit, a spiral staircase began to rise toward the ceiling. Stretching up seven decks, the mystic structure illuminated an otherwise dark ceiling until a neon sign appeared outside a sliding glass door at its apex: *The Crow's Nest.* Starting up the winding steps, Max noticed exhibits of seven world regions as he climbed. He staggered, somewhat seasick, around the first deck, observing sweeping panoramic scenes from Italy's Fincantieri Shipyard, showcasing a time-lapsed rendering of ocean liners flooding their berths. Welders assembled the final pieces of steel hulls as designers wrapped the finishing coats of paint around the bows and sterns. Christening ceremonies looped in the background as champagne bottles smashed alongside the departure of maiden voyages to every corner of the world. He stumbled up the stairs, dreaming about trekking to the farthest corners of the globe as he climbed above glaciers in the Arctic, waterfalls along the Amazon, cathedrals in Europe, and beaches in the Caribbean until finally reaching the entrance to the Crow's Nest.

This is just nuts, Max repeated in his mind. *I shouldn't be doing this.*

In the throes of his second-guessing, a young man dressed in a butler's uniform greeted him at the entrance with a steaming towel dangling from a pair of silver tongs. "For a bit of refreshment, sir," the man stated, his nose slightly upturned as if he too was second-guessing whether Max should be there.

"Thanks," Max said sheepishly. "Please, call me Max." Max gestured toward his clothes. "I didn't think my day was going to end up like this. Otherwise, I would've dressed more, well… like you. It's quite a… fancy boat."

"It's a ship, sir. Welcome aboard the *MS World One.*"

"Yes, of course. A ship. And really, please call me Max."

"As you wish, sir."

"As I said, I'm Max. Just plain Max."

"Maximum what, sir?"

"No, my name; it's Max Shades."

"My apologies, Mr. Shades."

"Max! My name is *Max*!"

Before the butler could respond further, a large, worn hand fell upon his shoulder. "I'll take it from here, Miguel. Thank you," the hand's owner said.

The butler turned on his heels to leave. As he walked away, Max watched a smile grow across the butler's face as if he'd been thoroughly amused by Max's sudden loss of patience.

"My apologies for Miguel. He has a strange sense of humor? We're happy to have you aboard, Max. My name is Henk. I'm the officer of the watch for *M.S. World One*."

Max detected an accent. A place from somewhere in Europe that had a lot of cold weather and schnapps. The man was tall and broad-shouldered with skin light on pigment, his hair no more than stubble on the sides while the top was a slicked-back streak of blond. His squared, clean-shaven jawline doubled Max's suspicion that he was from the Old World.

Like the snickering butler, his attire was formal. He was clad with an inky black, short-waisted frock coat layered upon a vest of the same color. The slack, golden chain of a pocket watch hung from the vest into a jacket pocket, and upon each of his shoulders were gold-stitched loops underscored by two bars of the same color.

He held his hand out warmly, waiting for Max to take it, but Max was still a bit stupefied as to what was happening. "I know it can be a bit overwhelming coming on board." Henk smiled. "It usually helps if I give a quick tour before I escort you to the Crow's Nest. Would you like that?"

"Uh, yeah. I mean, yes. Yes, please," Max replied. "If it's anything like the atrium, I'll think I've died and gone to heaven."

All around him were masterpieces, from the art hanging on the walls to the seemingly endless row of statues carved and polished from Sienna marble. The walls were plastered with richly stained mahogany that soared upward as if they were still trees.

Max stood mesmerized, slack-jawed by the beauty above the wood. Spanning high above them and as wide across was a dome of deeply stained glass. It arched like the window of a medieval cathedral that had somehow been curved and spread out. Its intricacy was breathtaking. Each piece of glass was soaked in green, blue, white, and brown tint. The collective shards told a story of brave, masted ships navigating the globe. Underneath their feet was a floor polished to a shine that reflected the glass better than a mirror. Max wobbled as he looked down. His knees nearly buckled as he recalled how he'd almost walked off the pier believing there'd been an invisible gangway. When he recovered both his balance and breath, it felt as if he was floating between two halves of a sphere.

"This is incredible," Max blurted. "I'm sorry, I just don't know what else to say."

"It's a beautiful reflector marble system, I agree. I suppose I'm used to it." Henk chuckled. "Compared to what you will be seeing, this is like white paint on a wall."

"That's not possible. I've never seen anything *like this*," Max said as he took another precarious step. It really did look like he was floating.

That is the beauty of this ship." Henk smiled. "Everything you see and do here will seem as if it shouldn't be possible.

It truly is a whole new world... There's more to come, Max. Now if you don't mind, please let me show you around the rest of our beautiful ship. Your new home."

"My new home," Max repeated. He liked the sound of that.

They passed through room after room of grandeur. It felt like a collision of antiquity with the distant future, like the galleries of the MOMA, the Louvre, and Hermitage were the inspiration for a space station. After Henk spent half an hour pointing out just a fraction of the vessel's interior, they arrived at the stoop of solid metal double doors.

Henk unsheathed his pocket watch, gently tapping a keyhole on the entrance. "This watch grants access to all public areas and events. All of the restaurants, shows, spa, map rooms, and so on. It is also your cabin key, so please wear it at all times. If you feel your watch vibrate slightly, then you're heading into areas designated only for the crew. It's nothing unpleasant, just a reminder."

"A reminder of what, exactly?"

"That you're a passenger, of course. This is a luxury vessel, and we insist on the crew meeting your every request, so please allow them to do so. Should you need anything, just ring the front desk."

Max liked the sound of that. He'd never been doted on and felt a tinge of excitement about ordering lobster and filet from the bathtub. "What's behind these double doors?"

Henk smiled. "Welcome to the Crow's Nest. I believe the captain asked you to meet him here?"

"He did." Max felt a flutter of anxiety. "Why does he want to see me, though?"

Henk chuckled at Max's visible worry. "It's nothing to fret. He always takes time to meet each new passenger."

"All of them?" Max questioned. During the tour, Max had seen scores of people touring the ship. No doubt there were hundreds of them.

"Yes, all of them. You'll find the captain is quite unique in that sense. And in other ways." Henk pushed open the door. "I'd join you, but like I said, I'm the Officer of the Watch. I'll see you when I see you... perhaps even tonight at the Welcome Ceremony?"

Max grit his teeth to avoid an improper laugh. "Sounds good to me. What's this evening?"

"It's when we spin the wheel."

Curiosity smudged Max's expression.

"You'll see what I mean later. Don't miss it. 8 p.m. on Roulette Stage. Now," Henk smiled, "let's not keep the captain waiting."

Max walked inside as Henk held the door open, fumbling for its handle while adjusting his eyepatch.

The room had no lights but was dimly lit, revealing a curved planetarium. Unable to distinguish the floor from the walls, Max gazed upon the twinkling panorama of constellations forming the figures of the zodiac above. As he scanned the room, a beacon of light shined down in front of him out of a gas lantern, projecting a shadow of scales upon a raised platform a few paces ahead.

"Libra," he whispered under his breath. The light receded, panning slowly away from his feet until it illuminated a wooden helm. He moved toward the wheel, grabbing the handles with ease as he confidently assumed control. Peering over its perch, the vast horizon of water lay beaconing before him. The sea was calm, quieter than he expected. Mesmerized by the vastness of the ocean and his union with this magnificent ship, he began to fade in and out of reality with each tilt of the wheel. Unable to contain his wanderlust, he fumbled for the watch in his pocket, desperately trying to set a heading, not knowing which Atlantic he was aiming toward, the ocean or the city.

"Easy on starboard, boy. Don't whip us around that quick or we'll shake off the stowaways." a stern voice whispered.

Max froze. Hands still gripping the helm, he glanced over his shoulder to find a towering figure draped in an orange-tapered leather peacoat. His wind-scorn face showing the trials of a thousand voyages. Beneath the wrinkles, a name tag flashed across his chest, barely visible from the dim lights in the planetarium: *Captain Lex.*

"Ugh, sorry sir. I-I was just, well... exploring?" Max stuttered.

"Give me one reason not to throw you off this ship, boy. Certainly a better attempt than free-spirited adventure, or I'll be casting you overboard to fend off the sharks on your swim back ashore." the captain taunted, concealing a smirk. "What the hell are you doing at the helm? Get out of the way." He brushed Max aside playfully as he regained control.

Feeling nauseous, Max managed to crack a response: "Well, you see, sir, I've been having these dreams lately, ones that keep repeating themselves, ya know? Premonitions of this magnificent ship, breaching the water above the horizon. Sailing into the Absecon Inlet. But just when it sails close enough to make port, I wake up. Frustrating, as you can imagine. It took a while to convince myself that your arrival was real!" Max confessed.

"Curiosity breeds trouble, my friend," the captain mused, running a calloused hand over his bristling gray beard. "But your heart seems to be in the right place." The captain leaned against one wall, staring up into the stars swirling over their heads. "When I was your age, I was haunted by similar dreams, dreams of a life at sea…"

There was a long pause, and Max wondered if the captain even remembered he was there.

Finally, the captain pushed off the wall and walked up to Max, who backed against the helm reflexively. The captain laughed, a brittle sound. "This life is in your blood, kid. Welcome aboard."

The room's lights began to flicker, and a thin green path illuminated the floor down a corridor from bow to stern. Max glanced over at the captain for one last reassuring farewell before making his way down the hall. The walkway stretched the entire length of the ship, just shy of 100 meters. Canvased paintings recreated oil-scenes lining the walls: landscapes vividly depicting prior voyages to every region of the world. Adjacent to each painting, an empty keyhole blinked a bright blue hue, peculiarly shaped like a pocket-watch.

Max fished his hand in his jacket pocket, ensuring the mythical watch was tucked safely away for when he needed it most, imagining the possibilities awaiting him just beyond these grandiose frames.

Upon reaching the end of the corridor, he encountered a large circular doorway with yet another blue keyhole. Above the slot, a sign reading, R017, began to flash on repeat as he drew closer to its frame. *Odd, I wonder where this leads?*

Placing his watch within the grooves, he opened the door and stepped inside.

What is this place? Max pondered as he sprawled out onto a king-sized waterbed, staring out his cabin window at the fleeting Atlantic City skyline hanging onto the horizon like a cat clinging to the edge of a building.

Overwhelmed by the embarkation, he drifted off into a deep slumber. Slipping deeper and deeper into a theta state of meditation with each rocking of the ship as it sailed farther away from port.

Bing, bing, bing, chimed a public address from the bridge.

"Good evening, and welcome aboard *M.S. World One*," a husky voice muffled through a static microphone in a thick, Dutch accent. "We are delighted you chose to embark. Please join us for dinner in our grand ballroom, Atlantis Hall."

The warm sting of reality broke Max's trance as he undressed. Numb from the abrupt departure, he hardly noticed the damp chill of his clothes still clinging to his battered figure like a winter surfer's wetsuit.

Shivering, he shuffled over to a corner closet, opening it to discover a wardrobe of prohibition era dress suits, commemorating Atlantic City's former glory in the roaring '20s.

Relieved, he dried off and donned a formal suit and tie. Shining his shoes and threading the last button on his shirt, he hoisted a cane from its holster and strutted down the promenade deck toward Atlantis Hall.

"Good evening, Mr. Shades, please follow me to your table," announced the maitre'd from the atrium.

Why can't he just call me Max? It's just Max!

The restaurant resembled a fish bowl. A transparent atrium stretched three floors, with circular seating in curved tables of nine seats. The centerpiece of the room showcased a thirty-foot grandfather clock swinging a heavy pendulum garnished with pearls. Max was escorted up a moving staircase, each step appearing and disappearing with each swing of the pendulum until he finally arrived to a chorus of greetings at a table with eight other passengers.

"*Buenas Noches!*" "*Wanshang hao.*" "*Buonasera!*" "*Bonsoir.*" "*Boa Noite.*" "*Dubry Vecher!*" "*Konbanwa!*" "*Guten Abend,*" the guests intoned warmly.

"Good evening," Max replied as he gracefully nestled into his chair. The room buzzed with novel interest in kindling acquaintances. Glasses clinked and silverware drummed across the tables. A quintessential symphony of sound resonated around the room as Max watched hundreds of fellow passengers exchange stories of their recent adventures.

"First day?" an elderly woman inferred, apparently empathizing with Max's wide-eyed expression.

"That obvious, huh?" he confided, attempting to uphold an illusion of comfort.

"I remember my first voyage," she reflected, tears forming in her eyes as the same spark of adventure invigorated her soul. "You're in for the trip of a lifetime," she imparted, winking tenderly as the grandfather clock ticked closer to showtime.

Two-by-two, passengers waltzed out of the hall. Amazed by the polished choreography of this grand departure, Max waited until the very last moment to make a move for the exit. Anticipating a cue, he rose from his seat and strolled out of the venue alone, gently closing its sweeping doors behind him.

Roulette Stage, Deck 2 FWD, a sign illuminated his path.

Following a bright green light lining the baseboards toward the bow, he emerged from the wings of the theatre just in time for the show.

"Welcome Aboard!" A familiar figure emerged from behind the curtain wearing an orange-tapered leather peacoat. "Kindly find your seats and place your watch in its slot on the armrest beside you. We hope you enjoy the show," a booming voice from the booth announced.

Lights dimmed, cueing subtle jazz music that underscored the space as Max took his seat.

"Welcome aboard *M.S. WorldOne*, where legends are set to bound. Our crew safe passage from port to harbor, the vision cast will sure be found," the captain continued, radiating a heavy timbre into a standing microphone. Electrical impulses sparked from its perch with every word.

"As we venture south to the warm waters of the Caribbean, ask yourself: what is so special about this place? Is it the sunshine? The beaches? The marine life? Or perhaps it's the people? The culture? The cuisine? Cast-away for wonder or plight, but be careful not to judge what appears at first sight..." The captain spun a massive roulette wheel that towered over the audience from floor to ceiling, showcasing a kaleidoscope pattern of flashing colors revolving around an excursion portal, highlighting their first destination.

"A toast!" the captain concluded. Raising a champagne flute toward the star-quilted ceiling. "To fair winds, swift seas, and limitless adventure for all those who seek!"

CULTURE CLASH

———

Tick, tock, tick, tock.

Max's pocket-watch began vibrating in the armrest beside him. He shielded his gaze from the intense reflection of a Caribbean sunrise glistening through the portal on Roulette Stage.

Along the horizon within the portal, an emerging sand-crescent island appeared with mesmerizing allure. Max imagined this tropical oasis had been a nourishing watering hole for generations of past explorers.

Henk's thick, Dutch accent over the intercom disturbed his reverie. "Today, you will have the opportunity to engage with an excursion of your choice. Follow your heart's desire, yet choose wisely, because the people and places you are about to encounter may set the foundation for a new life cast upon these radiant shores."

What have I gotten myself into? Am I really ready for this? Maybe I should just stay onboard.

One by one, hundreds of passengers rose from their seats and claimed a place in line along the wings of the Showroom. After what felt like an eternity, Max finally stepped up to a larger-than-life slot machine. The lever hovered over his head, daring him to set the wheel in motion. He placed his bet and pulled down the handle. A repertoire of excursions rolled in a blur and Max wiped the nervous sweat from his brow.

It's not too late. I could still turn back. Max checked his watch for a sense of comfort. Its hands read 11:11, pointing directly at the portal.

Mesmerized by the wheel, Max stared into the frame, spotting countless umbrellas tilting with the wind, shading luxury cabanas along teal beaches. Catamarans sailed through calm lagoons, their flags gracefully flapping in the peaceful breeze. Jet-skis sprayed salt showers on eager spectators along a thrilling obstacle course, while native islanders instructed their guests how to properly prepare jerk-chicken on open-flamed grills.

"Place your bet." the captain instructed, pointing at a blue keyhole resembling a pocket-watch aside from the wheel's lever. "How much are you willing to wager?"

Confused, Max asked for clarification. "I thought this was an all-inclusive boat?" *I can barely afford a beach chair, let alone a private cabana.*

Sensing his hesitation, the captain explained, "Your money's no good here, boy!" He shook his head impatiently. "We require something much more valuable, something finite, something that every passenger too often neglects to treasure."

This guy is off his rocker. How does he expect any of us to know what these riddles mean?

Max's pocket began to pulse. "The watch," he whispered under his breath. Reaching inside to retrieve it, he aligned its crystal case to the hole beside the wheel like a key. Clicking into place, the flashing light stopped while various scenes displayed across the portal's entrance.

"I'll ask you again, Max. How much are you willing to wager?" The captain tapped his cane on the floor to the rhythm of a mystic chant.

If my money's no good here...what else can I barter? Max fiddled with his watch in contemplation.

Suddenly, the answer came to him like fog-lights on a sunken treasure.

"Four hours," he claimed, winding his watch four times around its face as the minutes chimed and clicked with every revolution.

"Very good. Well done!" the captain chuckled.

Amused by the riddle, Max pulled the slot-lever down with all his strength as the scenes began to spin clockwise.

A mirage of excursions circled into view, finally landing on the vignette of a jet ski floating in a palm-tree-lined harbor. Glancing back at the parade of passengers inside the ship one last time, Max walked through the portal. Lights began to flash along a marquee-lined hallway as Max pressed farther into the fray. Turning around and around again, he struggled to see where one world ended and the next began as he finally emerged on the other side, seated at the controls of the fastest jet ski ever assembled in the region.

The sound of revved engines echoed in tune with a splash of cyclical wakes against the hull of each watercraft. Max donned a life jacket. He placed his watch on the ignition icon, and a sudden rumble beneath his seat spurred him into action. Hands gripping the throttle, he flexed his dormant strength with the sudden heat of hidden adrenaline bubbling beneath his skin. *What the hell am I doing? I can't compete with them!* he discerned, wobbling toward the starting line.

As he idled into position, a quick glance toward the shore-side pavilion rebounded an inauspicious glare from the local

Bahamian spectators, sizing up their competition. Dipping just under six feet tall, Max's staunch figure hardly won any bidders as he revved his engine within the daunting shadow of a Caribbean Goliath idling effortlessly beside him in the crescent-moon-shaped bay.

Is this a race or a boxing match? He gulped, overwhelmed with feelings of inferiority and doubt that quite literally triggered a sinking sensation in the depths of his gut.

"This is the notorious American racing champion?" scoffed the Bahamian contender, splashing him in his wake.

Checking his bare feet to ensure he wasn't taking on water, Max heard a distant echo of an announcer rallying the grandstands: "Welcome to today's main events, a cross boarder race for allegiance and territory. Place your bets and draft your contracts, for the stakes are much higher than bragging rights."

Contracts? Territory? I didn't sign up for this...

"Bang!" sounded the starting gun.

A capsizing wake rippled just behind Max's heading as a fleet of racers dashed forward into the course. *What the hell is happening?* Max stalled his jet ski, still dazed by his abrupt arrival to this tropical battleground. *One minute I was on a luxury ship and now this?*

"Get your head in the race, Max! We need you or we'll lose everything!" A teammate shook him out of his trance as Max throttled his engine and took off behind the lead pack.

A caravan of Bahamians swept the first three positions, while the lagging American rivals paced shortly behind, eager to turn the tide as palm-tree-lined runways faded to wind-scorn rocks outlining the narrow channel.

Max knew he needed to decipher the illusion of this tropical mirage from the trials of reality, if he had any hope of winning the race.

Steadily gaining positions around every turn, he tact-fully maneuvered inside the banks to fend off his opponent. Within three switchbacks, he penetrated the Bahamian lead pack. Shocked by his presence, they motioned a counter maneuver. Leveraging an imminent fork in the lagoon, they veered left, leaving Max to chart a right-bound pas-sageway solo.

I'll need to open throttle now, if there's any chance of gaining on them! With a quick view of the ship peeking through a coral arch signaling the final straight, Max leaned forward, slicing through the choppy current as he eyed the finish line.

"Quickly, mon, he's pullin' ahead!" the Bahamian leader yelled. Max split the flanking trio as they reconvened on the final stretch. Barreling toward the checkered flag, they inched closer, nose-to-nose. His eyes were blinded by the impact of the splashing water against an inbound current with only the roar of the grandstands signaling a proper heading. With one final push to edge his opponents, Max stood up and full-throttled.

Colliding across the finish line, there was no separating the two gladiators as their skis intertwined. Forged by fate, a rogue wave splashed into the grandstands, soaking eager spectators as they awaited the final results.

Paralyzed with confusion, the announcer managed to interject amidst the chaos: "We 'ave a draw! A truly remark-able change of events, for the victors are sure to claim to the contender's effects. Today is unprecedented. For no land shall be lost. The winner's prize must be shared, an experience gained at no cost."

Perplexed by the meaning of the remarks, Max noticed a green light beaming up from the ship's engine stacks in the distance. Suddenly, a loud whistle blared from the bridge as a portal reappeared in the water beneath his feet. With just enough time for a respectful glance at the Bahamian competitors, he flipped forward off his jet ski and into the portal, emerging back on stage from the other side as a swell of water poured out onto the reception, his clothes soaking wet from the transition.

One by one, his fellow passengers reappeared back through the portal, some clothed in tribal dress, others touting rum cakes, seasoning chickens, and juggling coconuts. Still dazed from his thrilling, high-stakes race, Max shuffled back to his cabin to process the day's events. Dripping wet and heavily fatigued, he nudged open the door. As he undressed, he noticed the strange presence of a foreign parchment rolled up on the desk beside him. He unraveled it slowly.

"Dear Mr. Shades,

Your timely visit to our tropical oasis came as both a blessing and curse for my people. Today's events left me puzzled by fate as our duel rendered no victor nor loser. I cannot fathom the fact that a feeble foreigner matched my skill on the water, and you've reluctantly earned the respect of my village. Our land is your land. As per the terms of our accord, yet your land remains to be explored.

Regards, Ashton

Max placed the parchment aside as he prepped a hot bath to relax. This letter came as no surprise, and he struggled to find the right words to describe the day's events, though he knew he must respond quickly. Decompressing under the surface of the salt water, the right response formed in his mind:

Dear Ashton,

Your words resonate politely from one culture to another, the thrill of challenging you is an honor in itself. Your land is not mine to claim, though let us reunite in time to share our adventures. My country is yours to visit, when the setting favors your arrival. For what I've learned, you are soon to uncover, our perceptions shift the more we discover.

Reaching for the parchment and a pen, he scribed the response on a blank space beneath the original message and cast it over the railing of his cabin balcony as *MS World One* sailed away into the sunset.

TOLLBOOTH TALES

"Ding, ding, ding," the announcement tone sounded.

"Good morning, this is your Captain speaking with the latest nautical and meteorological report. We are slowly making our way towards Gatun Lake, Panama in preparation to transit the canal. Our speed is ten knots across calm seas. We are expecting clear skies and sunshine, which makes for a pleasant afternoon on the pool deck. Whatever you decide to do on this relaxing day at sea, we hope you find time to reflect on our most recent port-of-call." he concluded, nursing a raspy throat as if he'd been rudely awakened one too many times to deliver this abrupt address.

Max laced up his trainers and propped open the door, peeking down the corridor for any signs of life. *Odd, why is everyone following the red markers today?* Dozens of passengers dressed in swimsuits, bathing caps, and flip-flops waddled down the hallway. Opposite the glowing red floor markers, a blinking green arrow guided Max along a different route. Swiftly rounding the corner, he paced up a steep staircase, taking steps two at a time, until he reached sliding-glass doors with an emerald sign etched into the terrace, *Fitness Centre.*

The space reflected shades of teal from the sea foam below, as light stretched through the windows. Spacious panoramas highlighted an approaching traffic tower as the ship floated through Gatun Lake, cuing up to pay a hefty toll to transit the canal and into the Pacific. Max paused, surveying the room as he stretched his arms and shoulders in search of the nearest weight rack.

"Hey, are you coming or going?" A staunch figure emerged from beneath a barbell, adjusting his eyepatch.

"Coming," Max responded, intrigued by the familiar tone. "Hey, Henk. Sorry, I thought you were a passenger." He relaxed his shoulders, exhaling a sigh of relief. "Well, I guess we're all passengers. Aren't we?"

"Depends. Some come and go. Some come and stay. Very few board and never leave. Guess I'm tryin' to figure if you're one of the some or the few." Henk assessed him out of the corner of his eye.

The ship's horn sounded as it approached the first lock, signaling an arrival into the canal. Machinery connected the bow to a tugboat while mooring lines gripped the hull into position for their first descent. Max moved swiftly toward the weight rack and hoisted the first load onto the bench.

"Spot me," Max prodded, acknowledging the serenity of their acquaintance as Henk dropped his curl to lift another disc onto the bar. "What brought you aboard, Henk? Where're you from?" Max laid down on the bench, beginning his first set, intent on listening for a response as a distraction from the load.

"I hale from Holland but consider myself a citizen of the world. Many of us nautical officers do. Being at sea most of the year, we start to call many ports home. My story isn't so different than the rest; I grew up in Amsterdam and attended maritime school in the south province, a port called Rotterdam."

Henk stuttered slightly between his words as if translating their meaning on the spot.

Reaching with both arms to add more weight, Max swapped positions with Henk as he glanced over at the nearest window: the second lock descended as the ship tugged forward through the canal, but suddenly, the landscape shifted scenes around the Fitness Centre to depict a massive port cityscape with dozens of vessels docked beneath an orange banner with a lion-crested insignia in the center.

"Ah, exactly, Rotterdam," Henk confirmed. "What about you? What brought you aboard?" he asked as they began their first set.

"I joined in Atlantic City," Max replied tactfully. "Your captain inspired me to stay. Guess he pitied the state of our town as you made port the other day."

Henk finished his set with ease, effortlessly re-racking the extra weight as the two exchanged places once again.

"Hmmm... were you the one running the beach as we sailed into port? Why weren't you gambling and shopping like the rest of your people?" Henk posed.

Breathing heavy with shaky arms, Max labored for the final rep. *I can't keep up; this bar is going to be the death of me.* The sweeping panorama of Rotterdam transposed into a Monopoly board around the Fitness Centre. Each street portrayed scenes of greed, lust, corruption, and vice. *Come on, Max, you're better than this. Push!*

He barely finished the final set as the panoramic windows reformed to depict the canal's third lock, inching the ship farther across the tracks. "My people are much more than blind gamblers..." he defended, springing off the bench to confront Henk's warped perception. "A little misguided, sure, but so much more."

Henk backpedaled as a glimpse of fear cracked his otherwise stoic expression.

Regaining composure, Max calmed down. "What do you say to a brisk cooldown jog around the observation deck?"

Towering over his figure like a solar eclipse, Henk was more likely to be spotted hand-hoisting an anchor than running in circles, but he agreed.

Stride for stride, the two seafarers trotted the outside deck, basking in the uniqueness of a bird's eye view of the events below.

"What did you do in the Bahamas?" Henk asked, as if embarrassed not to have thought of it sooner.

"I met some of the locals."

"Huh, interesting." Henk shrugged as he slowed down their pace. "I noticed someone racing a jet ski. It looked like quite the battle! I could hear the roar of the Bahamian crowd from the bridge, and it even rattled the glass window panes. We half-expected to leave the poor chap for dead as we pulled away from port! I feel bad though. Every season we lose a few passengers there."

"Like what?" Max inquired.

"Well, take yesterday, most excursionists lead groups to shopping malls or tourist boom-towns. A shame really, these passengers think they're experiencing the real destination, yet it's all smoke and mirrors," Henk revealed.

"Don't we have a choice? I mean, the roulette in the atrium cycles the excursions, but we don't have to take them, right?" Max asked, seeking validity.

"Well, not exactly," Henk continued. "The wheel does more than spin, and it's not entirely random. What really happens is the portal reveals the experience we need to conquer the most at that moment. It scans our soul and matches it with the right encounter, like your watch. It unlocks the path of destiny."

Max stopped running. Struck with revelation, he turned to gaze off the port-side railing, finally fixating on the obscure silhouette of a stormy character seated at the controls of watertight locks, directing the canal's traffic.

"Who's that?" he asked.

"Oh, him? He's the toll man," Henk replied confidently.

"Are you sure?" Max wasn't convinced. "Look at his stripes! He can't be the toll man. Is he one of us?"

"Ahh, sorry, mate. Yeah, that looks like H.D. Price."

"Price? What's his first name?"

"Beats me, I only know him as Officer Price. He's not favored here on board. A bit too entitled."

"What do you mean?"

"He always charges us for what should be free. You know, like the dinners and the excursions and the performances."

Max lobbied Henk for his periscope; he had to get a closer look at this guy. Retracting it slowly in the humid air, he finally focused its lens toward the tollbooth.

Seagulls squawked and circled the canal like vultures to a fresh carcass of roadkill. Beyond the chaos of their flock, the ominous figure stepped out on the balcony with a clipboard and a timepiece. He checked its hands religiously as if he patrolled the riverboat of Stix, ferrying condemned souls across the threshold between the living and the dead.

His sharp jawline cut across his pressed collared shirt so white that it made an oyster's pearl look like a worn dishrag. He labored to sustain his posture beneath the weight of an inflated ego, four gold stripes glistening in the afternoon sun.

Poised to impress a carnival of bystanders, the closer Max looked, the more fabricated they appeared. "He looks friendly," he scoffed, flipping the periscope back over to Henk as he fumbled the catch.

Pressing it up to his good eye, Henk continued to scout. "He's actually dressed down today. Normally, he's slipping into white gloves and a top hat."

Gloves? Top hat? This sounds familiar... "What's his story?"

"His story? What's wrong with you, Max? Do you live under a rock at the bottom of the sea? That's the heir to the infamous Price Empire. His family practically built your city!"

Max gulped, losing his footing with a rogue wake that rattled the hull as they drifted closer to the toll.

"Oh, shut up, Henk. Sorry I don't get my instant news from Twitter. I'm more of a newspaper guy. Real journalists don't tend to fuel the flame of some self-promoting basket case. And no, I don't live under a rock." He grabbed the periscope back in defiance.

Hoisting it up to his eye for one last glance, Max studied Price's movements like a reconnaissance jet in enemy airspace. His robotic strut and hand gestures mimed an open palm, demanding payment each time a ship crossed his booth. One by one, fog horns sounded as they were released from his grasp, casting away into the Pacific like orphans, robbed of their innocent childhood.

"Come on, we best wash up. Important night tonight." Henk gently retrieved the periscope from Max's grip.

"What's so important? Can't you see I'm still looking?"

"Well, no actually, only slightly. But I have seen your ambition before." Henk pointed a crooked finger at Price. "Come on now, Max, we best get going."

Tick, tock, tick, tock, gong! The clock in Atlantis Hall chimed as the last few passengers hurried to Roulette Stage. Captain Lex appeared behind the curtain in timely fashion as he checked the pocket watch in his jacket.

His stark figure paced just ahead of a trailing spotlight as he made his way toward center-stage. Staring at the production booth teleprompter, he hardly acknowledged the crowd before clutching a microphone to begin his remarks:

"Welcome back aboard *M.S. World One*. I'm aware we've recorded some changes to the passenger manifest since our last port-of-call. Please join me in welcoming our newfound mariners!" he said robotically, as if unfazed by their arrival.

A rumble of applause followed his announcement as the audience searched the room for their foreign companions.

"Allow me to introduce an old maritime sailing tradition." He grinned into the spotlight. "On days at sea, we welcome the chance to share our adventures from the region as we sail away from our Caribbean season."

Immersive displays of the tropics appeared out of thin air behind the stage. Grand visions of the landscape and inhabitants of a fantasy island that didn't exist on any map. Palm trees, coconuts, catamarans, rum barrels, and a restful village surrounding a peaceful oasis began to assemble behind the captain as he disappeared into the background.

"Take out your watch," a voice from the booth instructed in a deep announcer's tone.

Hundreds of audience members unsheathed their blinking blue dials, illuminating a dark theatre in instrumental sequence. Max admired the seemingly random light show, synced to the cadence of subtle background music as a spotlight focused on a microphone stand. He grew nervous, and his hands began to sweat, afraid that he'd be chosen to speak first. He covered his watch with a shirt sleeve, anxiously scanning the room for the first nominee.

Suddenly, the blinking symphony of blue extinguished, revealing a sole flashing signal from the second floor, port-side, balcony. A spotlight revealed the first participant, a short woman wearing a t-shirt and baseball cap lined with carelessly made glitter letters spelling out the word *Bahama* across her forehead and chest.

Unanimous but moderate applause echoed her footsteps down to the edge of the stage. A sense of relief radiated around the room as reluctant passengers exhaled nervous jitters when the captain reappeared onstage. She walked up the port-side spiral entrance to greet the captain as he handed off the microphone like it was a relay race. The woman fumbled the mic, barely catching it before it fell to the floor. Embarrassed by the loud screeching interference rebounding around the room, she collected herself before taking a deep breath.

"Ugh. Hi! My name is Annabelle, and I'm from the United States. I... well... maybe I should start by saying, I just wandered through a portal in the atrium yesterday and appeared in this tropical market."

Mystical landscapes formed behind her as she spoke, recreating the scene with fresh fruits, vegetables, and cheap souvenirs lining over-crowded streets, polluted with tourists. Seagulls squawked above filthy merchandise stands as greedy salesmen salivated through currency-framed sunglasses. The smell of smoke and rum stuck to every surface within a two-mile radius.

"I was searching for a gift for my husband, Rik. He loves baseball and always wanted to visit the Caribbean to explore the roots of Cricket and our Great American Sandlot. 'Annabelle, we need to take this trip, he pleaded. I *must* see the Cricket Museum,' he begged. So, for his birthday this year, we drove down to Galveston, Texas, hoping to catch a ferry to the island, where I encountered y'all! Just popping out of the water! Anyway, where was I? Oh yeah... I walked through the painting yesterday and wandered into this market looking for museum tickets when I got distracted by all the wonderful artifacts!" She motioned to the abstracts of souvenirs appearing on the screen behind her. "Then I got to thinking, whoa! This'll all be worth millions of dollars someday back home! Then coincidentally, a nice young feller with gold teeth handed me an empty plastic bag and complimented my outfit." She modeled a thick fanny-pack, high-tube socks, and white trainers.

"He said, 'Ma'am, you lookin' fine today, but how about you try yourself on the local suit?' Holding up this here combo." She pointed to her shirt and hat onstage.

Suddenly, thunderous applause sounded from the crowd. Glancing around to get a closer look, Max noticed most of the audience wearing the same outfit. *What a shame. Snap out of it!* he mused, more aware of their hypnosis with each passing minute as the monologue continued.

"Anyway, where was I? Oh, yeah. So I bought me $100,000 worth of these artifacts and the kind locals ushered me back to the gangway at the end of the strip. They even gave me this 'ere thank you card!"

She pulled a business card out of her fanny-pack. It read: *Thank you for shopping at Bootleg International. Here's a referral code for 10 percent off your next purchase of $250,000 or more.*

As she returned the card to her pack, a voice from the booth interrupted, "So what did you learn, Annabelle?"

"Well, I guess to seize opportunities for great shopping deals while you can! There isn't a sale every day! Gee, and what's even better is we don't need to pay taxes!" Just then, her face grew sad and cold, as if she finally realized the weight of her disappointment. Starting to cry, she ran offstage, disappearing into the mirage of failed pursuits behind her.

The jaded captain appeared from behind the curtain, head hanging low. "Okay, thank you Annabelle. Who's next?" The lights dimmed, revealing an auditorium of blue-flashing hues from a symphony of pocket-watches.

Max left his out from underneath his sleeve this time as the spotlight illuminated another speaker. A tall, well-groomed figure rose from the front row. His sun-kissed skin glistened in the limelight as he retrieved the abandoned, tear-soaked microphone off the floor.

"Good afternoon. My name is Daveed. *Gracias por darme la bienvenida a bordo.*"

A respectful, yet hesitant, round of applause greeted his introduction.

"A man walked into my showroom in search of an anniversary ring for his wife. As a diamond dealer, I was obliged to advise on the occasion. He shared the story of his marriage, how it was slowly deteriorating after many years of conflict, compromise, and bad blood. He loved his wife but always followed a passion for baseball more. His pursuit to unravel the origins of the game led him to the green pastures of England and sun-scorched midlands of the Caribbean. As we conversed, he began to confide in me. He realized that his lust for baseball would ultimately ruin his marriage, and he was committed to turn things around.

"'I wanted to treat my wife on our birthday to a little seaside getaway down in Galveston. So, we packed up our RV and set off on a drive down the coast.' the man confessed. 'It took everything in my power not to pack my 1996 vintage West Divisional Title Ranger's uniform, realizing that this was my last chance to show her how much I cared, before striking out for good. As we arrived, I couldn't believe my eyes. This magnificent ship breeched the water like some kinda Goodyear Blimp flying over a stadium! Determined to save the trip, I acted like I planned the whole thing. My wife, she was so excited! I just couldn't drive away, so we climbed aboard,'" Daveed reenacted.

"Invested in this man's pursuit to save his marriage, I walked over to our display counter and presented him with a pristine Tiffany engagement ring, set in platinum. 'Sir, if you are committed to turning your marriage around, you'll need to hit a home run, and here's your pinch hitter!' Mesmerized by its shine, the gentleman glanced up at me with unblinking determination. 'How much?' he demanded. '$125,000,' I replied. 'Sorry, man, I'm not made of silver and gold.'

"'I'll make you an offer, a trade if you will. Give me your watch to board this vessel. Swap lives with me for a year. If you still want the ring when I return, it's yours.'"

Max was on the edge of his seat. Mirages of the accord formed backstage as the audience clutched their arm rests in suspense of the desperate man's decision.

"You have yourself a deal," Daveed revealed, holding the man's watch above his head, revealing the name of Annabelle's husband, Rik, imprinted on the back.

Applause rattled the room as lights illuminated green markers on the floor, directing passengers out of the theatre. Climbing down from his vantage point to the walkway below, Max noticed some passengers disposing of their hats and shirts in a blue recycling bin during their departure.

ALASKAN ANGELS

———

Foxes are charming carnivores. Agile, yet cunning, they thrive on every major continent. Known for their intellect and sharp disposition, they discern truth with intuition.

Where are you going Mr. Fox? Max wondered as he stared at a snarling creature leading him into another portal on Roulette Stage.

Click, click, click, click, click, click; the slot machine turned as Max released its lever. A cycle of excursions rotated within the painting before him. Landscapes of snow-capped mountains, temperate rainforests, and eagles soaring between jagged peaks appeared through its oval frame. Removing his watch from its keyhole, Max took a deep breath and walked through…

"Step right up! Try a piece, or a leg, if you dare!" a show-man greeted wide-eyed tourists on the Juneau pier. *Tammy's Crab Shack* read the sign above an old fishing hut. Crowds of tourists swarmed his stand, splitting off massive legs of king and queen crab, hoisting them above their heads in a barbaric feast of spoil and glut, aloof to the miracle of fishery that retrieved this generous pot of marine bounty. Across from the crab shack, a neglected seafarers' memorial stood vacant; its overgrown landscaping lay untouched through the ages, silently commemorating hundreds of fishermen lost at sea in a treacherous quest to feed their families.

Float planes started their engines in the distance, taking off two-by-two as they ascended above the ship's docking position. Narrowly missing its smokestacks, they banked south out of the channel. Mist flowed down the enormous mountains, dominating the backdrop of the port below. Visibility weakened as mist turned to fog, gradually descending upon the jewelry dealers, textile vendors, and trinket shops.

Hundreds of foreigners rushed from storefront to kiosk, their arms overflowing with plastic bags, cutlery, fabricated gem stones, branded clothing, and promotional pamphlets highlighting the daily clearance sales. *It's as if the Grinch stole Christmas, brought it to Alaska, rebranded it as the North Pole, and sold it for twice the margins. What do these people plan to do with all this stuff they bought? It seems like their only motive in seeing the world is to consume, consume, consume. What is the point?* Shaking his head in disappointment, Max ducked away from the crowds.

He trekked up a steep hill where he could be more alone with his thoughts. Only the birds and squirrels seemed to notice as he hiked higher up the pitched blacktop, his forest-brown coat blending with the tree line surrounding him like a natural camouflage. Sound lagged behind his stride as the traffic of downtown subsided. Only the distant sound of rain and gentle gusts of wind occupied his senses.

"*Max,*" a mystical calling rushed past his ears, whispering gently as it swept into the forest.

What was that? He jumped, searching around for its source. Trees began to sway with the wind as the gusts blew stronger.

"*Max*," a voice whispered again. Louder this passing, as gusts traveled down the road ahead of him.

Rain fueled the valley mist, causing it to thicken into blinding fog as it consumed the town below. It ransacked the streets, extinguishing every light, sound, and transaction. The only thing visible was a green beacon projecting from the ship's bridge, indicating the position of the vessel to returning passengers like an ominous lighthouse, fatal if misplaced. His pulse quickened. *Am I going to make it back in time? Maybe I should stay closer to port...* Turning back around, a creature emerged from the fog. Its light brown fur faded to red as pointed ears perked atop his head. Swaying back and forth in unison with the trees behind him, its ears scanned the perimeter for disturbances like a detective dissecting a case.

The fox lurked closer, golden eyes locked on his. Max found he couldn't look away. Somehow, he felt connected to this small animal. The fox scurried toward an opening in the forest as Max followed shortly behind, feeling each step graze the roots beneath giant hemlock trees as if their paws and feet could sense one another.

Where is he taking me? I should really turn back...

Side by side, they ventured farther into the brush as the wind guided them toward an archway erected with two sculpted totem poles.

What are these? Max glanced over at the fox for reassurance. *Are they going to let us pass?*

The fox approached the base of the closest pole, sniffing the face that resembled a grizzly bear.

Careful, little guy... Max stepped over the fox toward the adjacent pole, inspecting the base for traps.

Anchored deep into the ground before them, the thirty-foot structure vaulted up to the canopy above. Identical animal faces mirrored each other as Max scanned their features from top to bottom, a grizzly bear, moose, salmon, and raven all stacked on top of one another like an ancient hieroglyph needing to be deciphered. The raven's eyes glowed bright green as they panned left and right with clock-like rhythm, patrolling the forest canopy like a watchful guardian, ready to expel wandering trespassers.

Pacing forward cautiously through the archway, the fox whisked its tail, signaling a clear path ahead. Max followed, crossing the archway and tiptoeing onto what felt like splintered wood.

Without warning, a flash of lightning blinded him, followed by an echoing crack that threatened to split his eardrums as a bolt struck a branch off a nearby tree. Falling to the ground, it began to smoke and ignite. Startled, Max jumped out of the way, shielding the fox from its sparks. Clambering over to the hazard, he grabbed the torn end, directing it away from his face as strong gusts of wind fanned the sparks into flames, crafting a makeshift torch.

Steadying his shaking arm, Max led the fox farther down the trail. The wooden planks beneath them creaked as he illuminated their path. Switchback after switchback, the pair trekked up the winding slope. *How long have we been at it? I can't go much farther... What are we even looking for?*

Max was startled by a low growl emanating from the fox's throat. He looked down to see it had stopped in its tracks, snarling. It scurried around a nearby boulder to investigate.

An enclave protruded from the mountainside. It's cold rock archway opened into a cliffside cavern, littered with chewed fabric, torn shirts, and cheap hats, Max could hardly find the proper footing to continue his climb. Struggling to find a route forward, he lit a path inside, noticing it stretched much deeper than it initially appeared. *We'll need to chart a path through. There's no other way.* Carefully following the boards beneath them, he couldn't help but feel the watchful eyes of a hunter hiding in the shadows.

"Stay close, I don't think we're alone," Max warned as the fox's hair started to tingle on the back of its tail. Gritting their teeth at the looming danger, the pair pressed farther into the cave.

"Turn back. You've helped enough. It's best I go alone," Max warned as he waved for the fox to flee.

Cocking its head sideways, it whisked its tail in defiance. Suddenly, Max felt the odd sensation of viewing the cave from the fox's perspective. Strange colors radiated from the quartz crystals embedded in the stalagmites below. Light reflected effortlessly through his retinas, illuminating a hidden path winding above the fractured rocks of a past earthquake as sunshine beamed through a hole in the stalactites above.

The fox snarled again as its ears perked to trace an approaching threat. Max froze. Breathing rapidly, he slowly pivoted around to the sight of a giant grizzly bear, dripping spit on his shoulders as it towered over them. Trembling in fear, Max felt the fox climb his back and perch atop his head, attempting to shorten the bear's jaw span as to deter it from swallowing them whole. Closing his eyes in surrender, Max held his breath as the prodding sniff of a wet nose grazed his chest. *Make it quick.* A disgusting drip of saliva from an unhinged jaw showered his face.

Suddenly, a mysterious gust of wind engulfed the cave, blowing a cyclone of sand and water to form an impenetrable barrier tight around the bear. "Spare the pair," it chanted, until the bear fled back into darkness. Half expecting to see the back of a grizzly throat, the pair opened their eyes and exhaled in unison, embracing each other in heartfelt relief. Shocked by their unbelievable survival, they climbed fractured rocks toward the sunlight above, collecting handfuls of onyx stones along their way to commemorate the near-fatal encounter.

Daylight broke the fog of yesterday as the pair pressed on. As they reunited with the boards of the main path, a sign post indicated: *Perseverance Trail, summit 1600 meters.* Exhausted from their trek, the sight of a nearby stream served as a welcome reprieve. Jogging over to the water's edge, they dunked their faces into the glacial runoff and began to chug.

Slap, slap, slap!

Lifting their heads from the surface, they rubbed their bruised cheeks in surprise. *What the hell was that?* Max gasped, chuckling at the scaly imprints left pulsing across the fox's swollen face. Brushing its sable beard against the moss of a nearby tree, its long snout twitched in confusion by the assault as it massaged away the pain.

Peering back into the current, they witnessed thousands of salmon in a military-like formation, swimming upstream to lay eggs. Stomach grumbling, the fox dove head-first into the water, resurfacing with three King Salmon in his jaws like an aspiring grizzly. Glowing with pride in his catch, he made a victory lap around a circular overlook.

Now he's just showing off...

Max followed, scavenging for kindling and flint to spark a campfire. The two sat side-by-side, gnawing on their lunch as they viewed the summit above. Its snow-capped peak captivated their attention more than any cable news broadcast ever could.

Revived by their feast, they continued up the switchback terrain on a final accent to the summit. *Home stretch! We're so close!* Max began to sprint to the top, the fox trotting closely behind him.

Reaching the peak, they collapsed on the ground, hyperventilating from the effort. After regaining their composure, they uncovered a stone podium with a familiar circular slot blinking a bright blue hue. Fumbling around in his jacket pocket, Max unsheathed his watch and aligned it with the keyhole.

The podium's surface retracted, unveiling a pair of crystal glasses. Max gently placed the frames around his ears as he peered through the lens, feeling as though he could discern truth from mirage with laser-like clarity as he gracefully paced the mountaintop.

A raven flew past them as it circled the summit, a salmon clutched in its talons from the stream below. Flanking their vantage point for three passes, it dove down the backside cliff and into what appeared to be a glacial ice cavern lining the valley beneath them. Mesmerized by its heavenly aura, the pair gazed upon the mighty Mendenhall Glacier as the sun began to set behind a distant mountain range. Its bright shades of blue glistened in the afternoon bliss atop a sleeping bay, undisturbed in a cradle of serenity protecting the region.

"*Max,*" howled the wind as darkness panned into the valley.

Intrigued by the invitation, the pair followed the sound down a jagged slope, surfing an avalanche of snow and gravel as they outpaced the sunset to the base of the glacier. Desperate for shelter, they frantically searched for a thawed cave to spend the night.

"*Max,*" the wind howled again as a rogue gust pushed them toward a lantern-lit alcove.

Bracing themselves for what was sure to be another savage encounter, they monitored shadows projecting from the flickering lanterns with unblinking anticipation.

"Caw!" The raven flew narrowly overhead as it glided into a cave around the corner, releasing its salmon dinner into a cast-iron pan. Strangely, the bird began to morph into the shadow of a woman, her short black hair blowing gently in the draft as she stretched gracefully into her new form.

Straightening his posture and clearing his throat, Max rounded the corner. Careful not to startle her with an abrupt entrance, he contemplated the best way to introduce himself. Grabbing a nearby icicle from the ceiling at the entrance to the dwelling, he extended his arm, poised to drop it on the smooth ground beneath him as a subtle disturbance to draw her attention.

"Best not to drop that; it's delicate," the woman suggested, her back still turned away from him, seemingly unalarmed by the presence of guests.

Max carefully laid the icicle on a table between them, appreciating the woven fabric of her black dress prominently displaying a quilt of laced feathers.

Back still turned, she instructed, "Place it in the pot."

Relieved by her hospitality, Max did as she said and stirred the icicle in a pot of boiling water at the center of a crescent-moon-shaped table made entirely of crystal quartz.

"Excuse my manners, but your entrance was quite, well, unique. Allow me to introduce myself, my name is Ma—"

"Max. Max Shades," she interrupted. "That your pet?" She motioned over to the fox.

Sniffing around the cave, he detected native tapestries, multicolor prayer flags, an assortment of ancient maps, chakra stones, smudge, and bags of mountain flowers with tools used to mince tea. A wide bookcase swept the perimeter of the room, holding shelves of ancient scriptures from every world religion. At the far end of the top shelf, a platinum canister flashed a blinking blue hue around a circular keyhole, far removed from the rest of the artefacts.

"More of a brother," Max replied, taking a seat at the table.

Kettle in hand, the woman turned around to join him. Her face resembled a beautiful bird, eyes big and bold, black makeup lining her expression as she blinked delicately through the steam rising from the pot between them. Reaching into the bag beside her for a handful of loose-leaf tea, she poured it into the pot. An aroma of mint, lavender, and chamomile filled the cave as the steam condensed into the glacial ceiling above.

"The name's Cera," she confided, taking a long sip of tea. Her polished gold fingernails tapped relentlessly on her cup.

Max took a shorter sip, mirroring her body language so as not to offend. "How did you come to live here? What's your story?" he inquired, attempting to hide his enthusiasm for her shape-shifting ability.

Breaking another icicle from the ceiling, she continued to stir the pot. As the water circled, shadows appeared in the rising steam, depicting the events of her past. A glorious ocean liner departed the Port of Southampton, England 108 years prior, the words *RMS Titanic* welded into the side of her hull. Fireworks ignited as it sailed west toward New York City in a magnificent Bon Voyage farewell. Scenes of extravagant events and intricate artwork transitioned into frame. Grandiose speeches and heartfelt performances were recreated in steam as the aura of abundant optimism and limitless adventure connected everyone onboard.

Suddenly, as the notorious iceberg ripped across the side of the hull, the profile of a young woman with short black hair and a feathered ball gown emerged on stage as her audience fled in terror of their looming demise. As the floating utopia began to sink into the Atlantic, the woman stood resolute. Holding a microphone center-stage, she calmly reassured her passengers not to panic and that help was on the way. As water flooded the showroom, a glimpse of her golden nametag revealed: *Cera, Cruise Director, RMS Titanic.*

Shadows dissipated from the steam as she poured more tea into the pot between them. "I'm just a nomadic intellectual, passing through the Northwest Yukon."

Unconvinced, Max pressed deeper. "What's that on the shelf?" He pointed to a golden nametag as the fox scurried over to snatch it for him to inspect. "You were a crew member? I thought you all perished?" he interrogated.

"Most, but not all." she replied, cringing at what was sure to be a lengthy interview.

"How did you survive? What was it like as the ship sank? Were you afraid? Why do you still look the same age? Who are the other survivors? Have you met them? Can they transform into animals? Have you been back on a ship since? Why—?"

Cera rose abruptly from the table.

The cave began to rumble and shake, as sounds of calving ice falling into a nearby bay echoed in the distance. Pacing over to the platinum box on her bookshelf, she fumbled with a watch in her pocket, its heading pointing directly at the blinking blue lock on the box's circular latch.

Clicking it in place, she removed the lock and retrieved a deck of cards inside. Dusting off their jackets, she began to shuffle. "Your arrival comes as no surprise, as the wind speaks to all those who are pure enough to listen." She paced back to the table. "However, our acquaintance wasn't met without a test." She artfully dealt the cards face-down as if prepping a game of Black Jack. Dropping her watch and nametag into the pot of simmering tea, she motioned for Max to follow her lead. "Place your bet." she announced as she shuffled the remaining cards; two lay facedown in front of him.

"I don't gamble on things like this," he declined, sliding his cards back across the table.

Stunned by his refusal and spiritual integrity, she flipped them over. "You're ready," she whispered after discerning their meaning.

Contrary to traditional decks of playing cards Max had encountered in Atlantic City casinos, these were no ordinary suits of hearts and clubs. The mystical patterns on their sleeves revealed a collection of ancient tarot cards. Curious as to what he drew as Cera interpreted, he studied the reflection of the cards in the ice ceiling above: a portrayal of a woman seated on a crescent moon throne donned a crown with a crystal ball lodged in its center. Beside her, another card depicted a hermit wielding a staff as he hiked a steep mountain, illuminating the path ahead with a bright lantern in an outstretched arm.

The alarming, cracking sound of ice calving drew closer, shaking the walls of the cave. "We don't have much time!" Cera warned as she poured one last handful of tea into the pot. Dipping his cup into the water for a final drink, Max felt a strange object brewing at the bottom. Ladling from the pot, he picked up what resembled a crystal microphone. Holding it above the brim as droplets evaporated toward the ceiling, the instrument glistened in the lantern light as he admired its craftsmanship.

Suddenly, the ceiling began to melt, and melt fast!

"Quick! Over here!" Cera yelled as the trio ran through a narrow cavern, ducking under low ceilings and dodging sharp icicles. Barely avoiding the collapsing passageways, they reached a dead end with a thin interior wall, deep inside the cave. Patting her feathered coat in a flailing search, she finally found a vial in her breast pocket and took a big gulp. She passed it to Max, and he followed her lead. After finishing the rest of the murky elixir, she transformed back into her raven form, desperately pecking at the wall behind them. Determined to help, Max called the fox, but it vanished from sight.

He glanced down at his hands, which were unrecognizable. They had become the smooth, red paws of his sly companion! A bushy white tail swayed behind him with every turn. Amazed at the transformation, he scurried over to the wall and began to claw, barely breaking through in time to slide down an ice luge and into the teal bay outside. The cave collapsed into the water behind them.

Swimming ashore to a nearby beach, Cera and Max regained human form. The fox was no longer at their side, but Max still felt its presence deep within his soul. Soaked and shivering from their epic escape, they wrung out their clothes in a hot spring nearby.

VIEWFINDER VICES

Eagles soared between the whispering peaks and pristine valleys of Glacier Bay National Park. Taking off from their nests like a fleet of reconnaissance jets, scanning the terrain for approaching threats to their homeland. Gliding in formation, they squawked in unison as *M.S. World One* breeched the surface. Her spotless hull waded in the wake of the sheltered fjord, calmly rocking back and forth while her ripples scattered toward the coast.

"That's my cue," Max remarked, winking over at Cera as she dressed.

Eyes fixated on the thermal pool, she hardly acknowledged his farewell as a green light shot out of the ship's smokestack.

Reluctant to leave, Max sat beside her, trailing his gaze into the pool.

"There's something you must see," she whispered.

Depictions of melting glaciers, rising sea waters, overpopulation, waste, materialism, and overwhelming greed formed before them. Lines of consumers waited to purchase tickets to hike a receding forest; airports filled to capacity with desperate travelers fleeing NYC, London, Amsterdam, and San Francisco. Sightless, soundless, expressionless figures wearing tinted glasses and over-ear headphones moved about aimlessly, blindly following their pocket-screens toward the latest product sold to the highest bidder. Families sent message requests to interact side-by-side, while couples rated each other's gestures through likes, dislikes, and emojis.

As the premonitions continued, Max began to feel sick. Simultaneous emotions of rage and despair compelled him to begin hurling rocks into the pool, relentlessly trying to end the horror film. As he hoisted the heaviest boulder he could muscle over his head, one final vision appeared through the surface, an old chalkboard magically etching the phrase *Do Something* in front of an empty classroom filled with rotting desks.

With one swift hurl, he splashed the boulder into the mirage, sending ripples over the edge of the pool and into the open water below. Trembling in anger, he dove in after it, emerging through a portal in the ship's atrium as the vessel reversed away from Glacier Bay.

A raven cawed overhead, circling the scene with a salmon clutched in its talons before disappearing behind a distant mountain range.

"More of a swim than a hike, I take it?" Henk snarked as he held out a towel. "You need to work on your showmanship."

Hundreds of passengers congregated to decipher why the atrium was flooded with ice, driftwood, and abandoned fishing nets, as a deranged man wearing crystal glasses lay star-fished on the floor.

"Sure beats the bus tour," Max snapped back, dodging judgment and further embarrassment as he staggered to his feet with the help of Henk's outstretched arm. Regaining his composure, he confidently deflected the remaining glares from posh bystanders as he limped out of the atrium.

"Who's the kid?" an ominous voice asked within earshot as Max clambered past a smokey jazz bar. It's dimly-lit mahogany rafters barely revealed a sign showcased in marquee bulbs, *Pinnacle Pub.* Slipping inside, he surveyed the scene from a discrete barstool. A cluster of indistinguishable suits queued to enter, each being scanned across the shoulders as they presented their nautical stripes like a bar code registering admission. Upon approval, they marched one by one toward a meticulously polished figure seated on a raised platform at the apex of the room. They nervously clinked cocktail glasses to greet him.

"Passenger 130668, *Shades,*" an advisor briefed, handing over a profile. "Joined in Atlantic City before the reposition."

"Keep a close eye on him," the figure ordered. A shimmering gold nametag revealing his identity under the burnt orange hue of Edison bulbs: *H.D. Price III.*

Ding, ding, ding.

"Good afternoon, everyone. This is your captain speaking with the latest nautical and meteorological report. We're making our way through the inside passage en route to Victoria, British Columbia with a SSE wind and favorable currents. Please join us on Roulette Stage at 15:00 for a recap of our Alaskan season before sailing south for the winter."

Thousands of cameras captured their last landscape image from the observation deck outside the showroom as passengers began filing into their seats, their faces still oddly glued to their viewfinders like tongues frozen to a pole. Max ushered himself toward the front row as lights dimmed again to reveal the familiar blue hue of watch signals flashing in sequence around the room.

How much memory can that thing hold? Max was unable to visually separate the woman from her camera as she stumbled up the stage.

Aside in the production booth, the captain briefly dug his head out from his hands for a strong swig of whiskey.

"Hello, everybody, my name is Shutter," she began, still staring at the audience through her viewfinder. "I didn't go ashore this season. There wasn't a place to charge my camera. But I captured a lot of photos of the—" She stopped suddenly.

What's going on with her? Can she even remember a single event without referencing her content collection? Max pondered, disappointed with her performance.

Frustrated, she walked off-stage to the sound of shutter flashes clicking from the audience. Reluctant to detach from their devices, the crowd sat silently anticipating the next participant.

Stirred awake by an unfamiliar weight in his suit jacket, Max felt the outline of Cera's microphone through the fabric. Reflecting on his narrow escape from the ice cave, he had an eerie suspicion of who would be selected.

Sure enough, as the lights dimmed and a spotlight searched the venue, it hovered above his seat. Taking a deep breath to settle his nerves, Max rose from his place among the masses and strutted across the stage.

Curious why he didn't have a camera pressed against his forehead, the audience grew quiet as they awaited the reenactment. Reciting milestones from his hike entirely from memory, Max captivated their attention as vivid depictions of his encounters appeared out of thin air.

"Fog rolled into the port... its thick haze blinding the horizon as the wind whirled through the maze of side-streets leading to the totem pole forest," he recounted, building suspense with each beat in the story, sparing no detail of his disdain for their consumerism. "I just couldn't take it anymore... your gross ignorance and pitiful sense of adventure!" *Whoa, this feels good... it's about time someone shook them out of apathy.* He decompressed, prancing around on stage to embody the narrative.

As the story progressed, murmurs escalated into mixed reactions from the crowd. Hesitant whether to continue, Max carefully concluded with a recollection of his view of the Mendenhall Glacier, concealing the events to follow. *I better not push it...*

"So, I reached the juncture of no return... scanning the dark cavern for a glimmer of hope as the grizzly lurked in the shadows." He gesticulated around the stage as vivid landscapes painted the scene behind him. "Narrowly evading death, the revelation of life infiltrated my consciousness on our final sprint toward the peak... finally! The last frontier! Free of your endless degradation and pollution!"

Unable to read the crowd through waves of applause, profanity, inspiration, and disgust, he scurried backstage just in time to avoid an arsenal of effects hurling toward his face. Watches, ties, shoes, necklaces, cufflinks, and other formal wear littered the stage as fights broke out in the grandstands. Although, amidst the chaos, more passengers chose to discard the remains of shattered cameras in their departure as they wrestled with the controversy embedded in his performance.

"Was it something I said?" He chuckled sarcastically, staring at his reflection in the dressing room vanity.

"Special delivery," Henk announced as he flung open the door. "Heck of a show, Max, really. Well done." he scoffed, tossing a red envelope on the desk beside the vanity before slamming the door behind him. "Do you realize what kind of position you put me in?" he yelled.

Still confused about the total impact of his speech but upset for obviously disappointing his friend, Max opened the envelope.

Mr. Shades, pack your bags in preparation
for disembarkation and report to
my office, N009, immediately.

H.D. Price III

Depressed and defeated, Max marched out of the dressing room, up the backstage steps, and down the corridor to his cabin, reluctantly stuffing his luggage for departure.

"Sir, please don't do this. He's new. He's still learning the ropes. He doesn't know what's at stake." Henk's voice reverberated down the hall as Max rolled his luggage to the doorstep of N009. Unsheathing his watch one last time to unlock it, he slipped inside. The room was meticulously designed, everything from the window drapes to the arm chairs were polished in a sleek black finish. A pyramid conference table, bolted to the floor in the center of the space, hosted six striped officers conversing amongst themselves as Henk continued to plead with the headmaster.

"You summoned me?" Max cleared his throat, sliding the red envelope onto the table.

"Ah, yes, Mr. Shades, I presume?" Price replied as he swiveled his chair away from Henk. "You've been quite disruptive lately... a bit too disruptive for folks in my position. We have a name for degenerates like you. Would you like to guess what it is?"

"Americans?" Max replied, as he sunk down into a chair, noticing a surrealist painting of a shark shredding the body of a seal to pieces.

"Shark bait," Price affirmed, holding back a smirk.

"With all due respect, sir, what have I done wrong?" Max posed.

"You're messing with things you don't understand, kid." Price scowled, looking back and forth from Henk to Max in contempt. "We can't afford to have your evangelical ideas corrupting the minds of our passengers. Who do you think finances this voyage, boy? Grandma Joan's trust fund? We've been sailing longer than you've been born. Things are the way they are. What makes you think you can change them?"

"I'm only reciting what I've seen, sir. Why punish me for sharing a different vision?" Max complained.

"Because it's the truth," Price admitted. "Luckily, we don't have to face it often, but we know what we have to do when we must." He pressed a button on his armrest, which opened a sliding-glass window overlooking the seafoam below. A wooden plank extended outward over the edge of the hull, seven decks above the waterline. *Well… looks like this is the end.* Max surrendered, accepting his fate.

A pair of striped officers gripped each of Max's arms and dragged him to the base of the plank. *There are worse ways to go…*

A raven circled overhead, swooping down onto the tip of the plank as it perched ahead of Max. Its black beak pecked the knots in the board, alerting him to turn around.

"Not this one, Price!" Captain Lex yelled as he slammed open the office door, motioning for Max to balance back away from the ledge.

"He'll sabotage our whole operation!" Price screamed, pointing his fingers in the captain's face.

"Maybe it's time for a change," the captain shouted. "Max! Return to your cabin. I'll have a skiff retrieve your effects."

Without thinking twice, Max hurried out of the room, eavesdropping on the quarrel as it echoed down the corridor until eventually fading out of earshot. Reluctant to return to his cabin, he ducked into the Crow's Nest to process what just happened.

Approaching the helm under a starlit ceiling, he noticed a bookshelf opposite the wheel across the room. Its ornate curvature depicting classical scenes from antiquity as it wrapped around an assembly of leather chairs and interactive wall maps. Studying the blinking dot representing the ship's position moving flawlessly into Victoria Harbor, he contemplated the prospect of disembarking on his own accord, frustrated with the politics of tradition governing this floating city.

"Forget it, I'll just move to Alaska," he daydreamed, recalling the untapped potential and lush rainforests of Juneau and the serenity of solitude experienced along his hike. *No superficial commercialism, inflated egos, and shallow hierarchies there.* Turning back toward the bookshelf, he envisioned retreating to the vast wilderness of this final frontier, studying for a law degree, and retiring as a transcendent hermit like Cera had many years before.

Stomping toward the exit, he noticed a peculiar pamphlet stored in the classics section: *Common Sense* by Mr. Thomas Paine. Recognizing its title from school, Max extended an arm to dust off its bindings when his hand abruptly connected with someone else's through the back of the shelf.

Shocked and intrigued, he pushed aside the rest of the books to catch a glimpse of the mysterious intruder. Hands still gripping both sides of the pamphlet, reluctant to detach, the pair locked eyes for the first time.

"See anything you like?" Max asked, referring to the books.

"Yeah, a few," a woman responded softly, her big bedroom eyes and gorgeous smile gleaming through the shelf as Max stumbled backward, surrendering his grip.

Heart racing and palms sweating, he felt an overwhelming desire to understand this chance encounter. As he glanced back through the shelf for a closer look, she disappeared, spinning around the corner to greet him in 4/4 time like a professional dancer. *Who is this woman?*

"Do you work here?" she prodded, clacking her Italian leather shoes on the tile beneath a classy cocktail dress. "What's your function?"

"Depends on the day... and what you define as work," Max replied, rattled by her confidence and intrigue. "I joined as a passenger a little while ago, but now I'm not so sure." He finished with underlying uncertainty, heart racing with overwhelming attraction. "What about you?"

"I'm a performer. Just embarked today," she revealed, shuffling through the pages of *Common Sense*. "We have our first show this week. You should come watch!"

Why is a performer spending her time in the classics section of a library, of all places? He regained enough composure to articulate a steady response. "Yeah, sure!"

Yeah, sure? That's all I could come up with? Come on, Max, keep it together...

Mesmerized by her aura, the thought of jumping ship for a life in Alaska suddenly felt devastating.

"Wait!" Max called after her as she strutted toward the exit of the Crow's Nest. "I never caught your name."

"Ella," she shared swiftly, spinning out of the room.

INTERNATIONAL RELATIONS

———

"You won't get far with that tongue, kid," Captain Lex reprimanded. "Are you trying to cause a mutiny?"

"No, sir. Sorry, sir," Max confessed, slouching deep into a chair in the captain's office.

"The fact you aren't split to pieces chumming the water is beyond me. Price is ready to cast you away."

"I want to be here, sir! Everything feels so clear now!"

"Well, start falling in line. I can't keep bailing you out. We should've left you to die like your pitiful mirage of a city."

"Watch it!" Max clutched his fists at the insult, teeming with rage.

"Show some damn respect, son. You wouldn't last five minutes working the docks." The captain scowled. "You've got grit, kid, I'll commend you for that. But you need to be more diplomatic if your goal is to inspire." He motioned toward the door. "Get out, before I change my mind."

Stomping out of his office, Max punched a hole in the wall of a nearby corridor as he retreated to the promenade deck.

"So, then I toured the Southwest, chartered a bus to L.A., and made it just in time for the opening number," a soft familiar voice said as Max rounded a corner.

"Whoa, something similar happened to me in The City. I freaked out and had a panic attack before our final call," her friend replied in a harsh New Yorker accent.

"Like, OMG, me too," another shared in an Australian twang.

"Oooh, you made it though! Bish, Bash, Bosh," an English pitch applauded.

Max trailed their voices to a group of performers buzzing around a set of lounge chairs. Their tight circle of gossip stewed in a low simmer, muffled by the humming of engines as they ventured farther south off the coast of Mexico.

Great, there're more? This is trouble. "Umm, good afternoon, ladies. Welcome aboard!"

He was met by a chorus of giggling as the girls turned to watch his approach.

"Why, helllllooo, thanks." The Aussie blushed.

"Watch it, punk!" the New Yorker defended.

"Hey, Max." Ella gestured, reassuring the others.

"Hey, Ella, nice to see you out and about." His voice cracked under the pressure of her greeting. "Have you been up to the observation deck yet? May be a good place to start getting acquainted with the ship."

Geez, did I forget how to speak? What's going on with me?

"No, we haven't. Thanks, though! What brings you out of the library?" She posed, twirling her hair with a shaky finger.

"Needed some fresh air," he replied, awkwardly shifting back toward the railing.

Suddenly, a whale breached the surface of the seafoam below, gracefully waving at the group before dipping back down beneath the waves.

"Oooh, look at that!" Ella darted over to the railing, nudging him aside as she pointed at the surface, attempting to claim credit for its appearance. "Girls, girls, look! Did you see that! It waved at me!"

Using the opportunity to dodge an extended engagement, Max slipped away to continue pacing the promenade. "Good luck tonight!"

Unfazed by the spectacle, Ella's gaze lingered a bit longer as he stumbled away from the group. *Why is she still looking at me like that?*

Clunk

A lifeboat lowered alongside the railing. Its bright orange paint branded the number two across a buoyant hull as a ramp connected it with the promenade deck. *Here's my chance; it seems to have enough supplies for a week at least.*

Walking inside to take inventory, Max caught a glimpse of Ella through the pilot window. Fumbling with his watch on the lowering hinge, his hands shook with indecision. *What if... maybe, just maybe...* He debated, hands seconds away from dispatching it into the sea.

Retracting his watch from the controls, he slammed the paddock doors shut and rolled the ramp back into the boat, securing its hooks and hoisting it back into storage overhead. *This is stupid. I should be miles away by now.*

Conflicted, he lapped the deck in contemplation for the next few hours before retiring to his cabin. *I can't let this go on much longer. If I stay, things need to change around here.*

Ding, ding, ding. "Good evening, everyone. This is your Captain speaking. As we make our way south of the equator over the coming days, we invite you for a featured performance tonight by our newly embarked singers and dancers."

At least he's not highlighting the Alaskan clearance sale.
Max staggered to his feet, donning a black suit and tie as he
scurried down the corridor toward Roulette Stage.

"Ladies and gentlemen, welcome to tonight's premiere
event! Please put your hands together for the performers of
M.S. World One!" the captain announced.

Thundering applause rocked the ship as it listed back and
forth to the rhythm of entrance gongs.

Why is everyone holding a fishing net? Stumbling over
empty pails and baited hooks, Max climbed into his seat next
to Henk. A row of striped officers sat polished nearby, fishing
rods in hand, they cast their lines onto the stage, hoping to
hook a performer with their status and inflated charm. A
medley of chart-topping hits shuffled throughout the performance. Costume changes cushioned the transition numbers
as the cast portrayed music from every decade.

Evading Henk's shallow attempt to catch a performer,
he nudged his shoulder in disgust. "You're better than this,
mate. Where's your sensibility?"

The dancers whisked by in unison, preparing for an
aerial routine.

"Oh, I'm sorry, at least I have a filter," Henk fired back,
still fuming about defending him from Price.

Act I ended with a sweeping acrobatic number of dark erotic
tangos, leaving most of the audience sweaty, relentlessly reeling in
their lines and recasting them, hoping to catch a dancer, or two.

"Where's your head, mate! Grab this!" Henk handed Max
a harpoon.

"I'm fine on my own, thanks," Max responded, watering
can and fertilizer in hand.

"This is your chance! Don't you want one of these fresh
catches?" Henk asked.

"It doesn't work that way, Henk," Max explained. "What are you here for?"

"A woman, scantily clothed, prancing around upstage like that only wants one thing," Henk affirmed.

"Oh, yeah? And what's that?" Max gritted through his teeth, gripping his armchair to avoid punching him in the face.

"Let's hear it for our talented group of performers!" the captain interrupted over the loudspeaker.

Setting aside their differences, Henk and Max stood up to applaud the final act.

Who's that flower in the mirror? Max followed a fleeting dancer to the edge of the stage. Her big beautiful eyes gazing back at him with tunnel vision, as if the world had stopped spinning. *She's gorgeous.* He daydreamed, sharing a moment with her in timeless serenity as she took a bow before disappearing behind the curtain.

Dusk turned to dawn as the evening faded with the fog along the sunrise horizon.

Max dug a hole in a garden lining the observation deck, reflecting on the turmoil littering the audience the night before as fish nets, harpoons, and empty pails floated away from the seafoam.

How long will these take to bloom? He sifted through seed after seed of roses, as he planted them in the spring soil.

"You keep digging like that, and you'll hit buried treasure," Ella said softly, as she started watering the flowerbed beside him.

Startled by her sudden appearance, he kicked over a bag of fertilizer. "Damn it! That's too much." *Come on, Max, keep it together. She's just wandering around the ship.*

"Oh, it's fine, look. See!" Ella spread handfuls of dirt from the middle around the edges, ensuring not to neglect any thin patches.

"Yeah, I guess you're right. Best to spread it out more. Wouldn't want to overload a few seeds." He nodded. *She's on to me. Why do I feel like a flailing toddler everytime she's near? How could she possibly think I'm playing it cool?*

"Thanks for coming last night! Did you like the show?" she asked, raking a mound of soil a bit too many times.

"You're incredible. The choreography, music, costumes, lighting, set design... It's all very inspiring." He attempted to mimic the tango steps with a nearby shovel as a partner.

"Well, you've obviously learned a few numbers." She applauded. "What's this fascination with gardening? Aren't you more of a sailor by now?" Her eyebrow raised in suspicion.

Great. She thinks I'm one of those eager deckhands. "Well, I just feel it's best to plant your seeds and watch them grow for everyone to enjoy. Roses are my favorite since their roots run deep and petals wilt then bloom over and over again. It's like a cycle, you know? You plant one seed, give it enough water, and look!"

A stem of roses grew out of the garden before them. Their white and red petals bloomed faster than any bush could back on land.

"Well, you certainly proved your point." Ella held back laughter as she stood in bewilderment, taking a long sniff of the biggest flower.

A swarm of bumblebees landed on the bush, gracefully pollinating the flowers as Ella dodged their descent. Slipping on her backpedal away from the garden, she fell into Max's arms.

"Hey! Would you fancy a night out?" She gazed up at him in admiration. "The cast and I are going to Bingo later. Would you want to join?"

Bingo? Really? Of all the things to do on a day at sea, Bingo? Smirking at the invitation, Max tried to muffle his reaction. *I'd do almost anything to spend more time with her.*

"Bingo sounds fun! Thanks! But maybe after, we could go for dinner?" he posed.

"It's a date." Ella nodded, spinning down the steps from the observation deck. Her pointed toes glided across each plank in a weightless trance.

His heart pounding him into a state of reverie, Max admired the beautiful garden they'd planted, already teeming with life for everyone to see.

"I guess that's how it's done?" Henk called out from the bridge, unloading his harpoon and fishing gear over the railing as he jogged across the observation deck.

Couldn't I have picked a more discrete friend than the Officer of the Watch? "Hey, Henk. What do you mean?"

"Hooking a performer, of course! Well done, mate!" Henk knelt beside the garden, planting the last handful of seeds in an empty row of soil.

"For someone who watches everything, mate, you really can't see a thing, can you?" Max shook his head slightly before climbing down the stairs toward his cabin.

"B-7... B-7," the announcer called. "G-2... G-2."

I can't believe I'm sitting through this. Max scanned the room, searching for any distraction from the monotony.

"Oooh, you're getting close!" Ella applauded, glancing over his shoulder at a marked Bingo card.

"No, he's not. Why did you even bother inviting him?" the New Yorker scoffed.

"Because he's wearing an adorable bowtie," the Aussie teased in response.

"Hush up!" Ella defended. Sliding her hand across his armrest.

Meeting halfway, Max wrapped his fingers around her knuckles, squeezing palms for the first time. *I can't believe I'm sitting through this.* He was absolutely stunned by the sensation.

"Bingo!" a participant yelled, running up the aisle toward the draw table.

Hands still locked, the pair cleared their boards. Neither was willing to let go of their embrace amidst the obvious struggle to reset their chips.

"Hey, I have a good feeling about this," Max whispered in Ella's ear.

"About what?" she whispered back.

"This next round. Here, switch boards with me."

They swapped cards, sneaking a glance of excitement in each other's eyes as the numbers cycled.

"B-4... B-4." The first corner of Ella's board.

"I-5... I-5." The second corner hit, and Ella's grip tightened around Max's palm.

"N-1... N-1." Unbelievable. Three out of three.

"G-7... G-7." Another corner covered.

"O-2... O-2."

"Bingo!" Ella celebrated, dashing up to the draw table in victory. Picking up her prize, a dinner for two, she rushed back to her seat in shock. "How did you do that?!" she demanded, poking Max in the shoulder as if he staged the whole thing.

"I told you! Just had a good feeling about it is all!" he repeated.

"You've got to be joking," the New Yorker said with a shake of her head.

"Whoo-hoo! Alright!" the Aussie celebrated.

"Dinner's on me tonight." Ella winked, still buzzing with excitement as she hugged him.

"Alright, we'll catch you later, girls!"

Pacing out of the room, still holding hands in disbelief, the pair made their way toward Atlantis Hall.

"Good evening, Mr. Shades. You're looking marvelous! And who's this dainty little flower? A newcomer? Oh, wonderful." the staunch Maitre d welcomed them through an archway of the main dining reception. "I sense a special flare with you two. Come-come now, but where to put you?" He shuffled between the tables like a xylophone player crossing arms to play scales between octaves.

"Oh, thank you —" *Ah, what was his name again? Damn. I should've remembered from embarkation night.* "— Klaus." *Whew! Thank God for nametags.*

"*Ausgezeichnet!* Such a wonderful booth, tucked nicely away from the chatter." Klaus guided them to it. "Follow me now, yaa?"

As they strutted down the carpet, Ella's hand still rested in his embrace as the pair glided toward their seats alongside the window, causing whiplash for hundreds of guests as they eyed her gorgeous gown and delicate curves. *What is everyone staring at? Haven't they seen a golden bowtie before?* Max thought foolishly, basking in the shadow of her figure.

"Ah, here we are. Perfect." Klaus announced, extending a chair behind Ella to sit. Her sequined green gown reflected light off the chandelier above.

"You're beautiful," Max complimented, as if her formal facade made no difference.

"Why, thank you. You clean up nicely yourself!" She blushed, nodding at the words of affirmation. "Sorry, but

I ran out of makeup after the show." She shrugged, slightly embarrassed by her naked face.

"Any more and you'd be fake." *Hope that wasn't too harsh. Yikes.* He reached for her chalice to pour her a glass of wine. "I prefer you without, honestly."

"Really? Most guys expect it from performers. You know… always dolled up and laced." She sighed, as if accepting the stigma.

"Not everyone can separate the art from the artist," he affirmed, slightly embarrassed.

"Yeah, exactly!" She relaxed, dipping a roll into a stick of butter. "Hey, what brings you aboard this —"

"Good evening, madam, Gentleman. Welcome to Atlantis Hall. My name is Gus, and I'll be your waiter. We have a delectable spread of fresh fish from our Alaskan season along with succulent steamed vegetables, braised couscous, and creamy tiramisu for dessert. What shall I place for you—?"

"Salmon," the pair responded in sync, not wanting to waste another minute of conversation.

"Of course," Gus noted, sensing their intimacy as he darted off to the kitchen, improvising their order along the way.

They stared back into each other's eyes.

"I joined awhile back, in America," Max replied with subtle embarrassment of his nationality. "Just south of New York City, along the coast. I can't explain what happened, or why me, but this recurring dream led me here, to this magical ship. Endlessly sailing across borders and cultures. No city… no place felt right… except for here." *With you.* He bit his tongue to hold back the words.

"America? New York City! I've always wanted to be a Broadway star! I played Princess Jasmine, you know."

Princess Jasmine? I'm starting to feel more and more like Aladdin.

"What's England like? Do you really drink that much tea? I'm more of a coffee guy." He snickered, steeping a bag of Earl Grey in the kettle.

She rolled her eyes. "You're more of an Englishman than you realize." She pointed toward his perfectly stacked tower of bread all to one side of the plate.

"England is lovely." She crossed her legs beneath their table. "We have big, rolling hills of farmland with gorgeous gardens. Cheeky gin and tonics, lots and lots of trains, fancy castles, and Christmas. Christmas is a *very* big deal in England. As for tea? I have a cuppa PG Tips here and there, just a splash of milk and maybe a little honey, but most of our tea comes from China. Especially through Greenwich in the Port of London!"

Sounds delightful. I can almost feel the grass beneath my feet, walking around Hyde Park in the spring. Tossing a stick to a yappy terrier on a Sunday afternoon. He turned to day-dream out the window. The gentle splash of seafoam washed the glass. *What does the future hold? Am I destined for a life at sea? Floating between countries and continents for the rest of my days? Am I fit to return to land? Will I be happy?*

Turning back from his visions, he placed his hand in Ella's across the table. Their gentle embrace triggered overwhelming feelings of love and commitment as the clock anchoring the hall stopped ticking.

"Have you always wanted to be a performer? What are you planning to do when your career is over?" he asked, as their dinner arrived on silver platters.

"Well, yes, actually. I've always been drawn to the theatre. Acting, singing, dancing. All of it, really! I can't imagine being happy anywhere else." She lifted the cover to her dish. "But over? What do you mean? I'll never really retire. There's always a place for entertainers." She sounded slightly offended.

"Excuse my ignorance, I was only curious," Max apologized. "It's not often I meet someone so... unique." He removed his cover to garnish the fish. "Most of my friends went on to... Well, more normal careers."

"Like what? What did you want to be when you grew up? Actually, better question, what *are* you doing for work?"

Taking a big sip of wine, he mustered the confidence to respond. "Well. You see, I was kinda like a performer growing up, except on the track. You know, running, races, big arenas, and flashy personalities. I couldn't imagine retiring to live a well, *normal* existence: cubicles, phones, emails, copy machines, conference rooms, etc. I thought about becoming a lawyer or politician or a teacher, but no role really inspired me, you know?"

"So, you're unemployed?" She cringed, driving a knife through her fillet in anguish.

Great, now she thinks I'm some penniless recluse scurrying through the slot machines. "Well, you can say I'm in transition," he clarified, feeling the imprint of Cera's microphone still tucked away in his suit jacket.

A toddler at a nearby table wailed and dropped her toy from a highchair.

Kids? Great, this is not the impression I'm hoping for on a first date. Max tapped his foot in discomfort.

"Aww, look! She's like a little Dora the Explorer." Ella glanced over at an officer and his wife as they comforted their little girl.

"Madam, Sir, your tiramisu," Gus announced, clearing their plates as he reset the table for dessert.

Picking up a spoon of whipped cream, she playfully flicked it at Max's face and it landed on his nose. "You could be a clown! There ya go! Let me have a look at you... yup!

Someone book this headliner! Guest Entertainer, everyone, here he is!" she yelled, attracting unwanted attention from striped officers across the room.

Blushing, Max wiped his face. "Yeah? Or how about this? Poof!" He pulled a dove out of his sleeve, gently releasing it out of the window as it flew away toward the California coast.

"Oooh, a magician! Yeah, there you go! Can I be your assistant?"

Patting around his pockets for another prop, he found the only thing left was the microphone. "Or there's this?" He revealed its crystal design, reflecting light from the chandelier as it sparked.

"Whoa, yeah. That suits you. You have a beautiful speaking voice. You know, we could use someone to intro our shows, maybe highlight a few events around the ship. Do you fancy monologues? I'd much rather see you up on Roulette Stage than crinkly old Captain Lex," she suggested, eyes wide with enthusiasm.

Reflecting on his controversial first performance, Max shrugged. "I don't think our passengers would appreciate my slant on things." He slid deep into his chair as if trying to absorb into the upholstery.

"Nonsense, Max! You're perfect for that role!" she rallied, nudging him out of complacency.

Do I really want to rock the boat... again? Price will have me cast overboard to fend off the sharks if I step out of line.

"Come on. Let's try to catch a glimpse of the moon before the clouds roll in," he deflected, rising to leave.

The clock began ticking again as its large pendulum swung beneath many faces, counting every time-zone from Greenwich to Samoa as they made their way toward the promenade deck. Just before reaching the outside terrace, Max overheard a pair of striped officers whispering under their breath. *What's that about?* He cut a corner to evade further surveillance.

NAUTICAL NOSTALGIA

"Max Shades, please report to the Crow's Nest immediately."
The captain's announcement broke the early morning silence
blanketing Max's cabin.

He must be the earliest riser onboard. Max stirred, clambering
around the room in a haze, wrestling with his morning slumber.
I wonder what it is this time? Shoes still untied from the sudden
summons, he flung open the door and tripped down the corridor.

"Ah, just the man I wanted to see," the captain greeted
him, leaning against a bookshelf.

"Good morning, sir." Max shuffled into the nearest lounge
chair, still half-asleep.

"You know, son. I've been thinking a lot lately, about our
passengers and this voyage. When you reach my age, you
think you've seen it all! The world, and the cultures that make
it come alive." He shifted from the bookshelf to a large globe
in the center of the study. "You start to, well... repeat yourself.
Reciting the same monologues, introducing the same shows,
and sailing the same itineraries year after year."

"Sounds like you're giving a farewell address. Are you
finally going to retire?" Max inferred, searching the room
for a cup of coffee to break the morning slump.

"Finally? What do you mean by *finally*?"

"Well… I mean to enjoy your golden years."

"That's what I thought you said." The captain scowled. "I'm not retiring. No, never. But I do need someone to take over certain duties."

"Like steering the ship?" Max finally found a cup and perked up.

"Nice try," the captain snapped, stroking his beard in contemplation. "The passengers need someone they can relate to. Someone who can advocate for their journey. Someone—"

"—younger?" Max interrupted.

"Quiet, kid! Damn it! But, yes, younger."

"Well, what about this whole diplomacy lecture? I thought you labeled me a renegade, a recluse? An instigator?

"We talked about that. You just need some time to rehearse. To learn a few more things." The captain slid back toward the bookshelf as he handed over excerpts of passages from Cicero and Sinatra, Larry King and Oprah. "Here. Have a look through these." He slammed a stack of books on the table between them. "It's a start."

"Thanks, sir, but what exactly do you need me to do?" Max flipped through the pile.

"We need a Master of Ceremonies."

"You mean like an MC?"

"Yes, is that what the kids are calling it these days?" The captain rolled his eyes.

"Why me? Have you asked one of the performers? They have a better sense of showmanship."

"Well, it's more than just putting on a good show. You're really the head diplomat. The mayor."

"But you think my message is too controversial? Too disruptive?"

"We need someone who can really embody the needs of the passengers and crew. Even if that's a bit… rough at times."

"I don't know, sir. I considered jumping ship in Alaska. Do you really think I'm ready?" Max crossed his arms, sinking deep into a leather chair next to his stack of homework.

"Talk to me about this new flame?" the captain mused, smirking slightly.

"Flame? What flame?" Max denied, attempting to dodge the looming interrogation.

"Everyone saw, Max. Don't play dumb with me. You're inseparable."

"Well, Ella… She's… she's inspiring." Max's voice cracked, face red with embarrassment.

"Ella? Hmmm. And she's a performer, right?" The captain began leading him through a thought experiment. "And she's comfortable on stage?"

"Yes, I suppose. Yes."

"And she knows how to work a microphone?"

"Why, yeah. I guess so."

"And she's in rehearsal right now probably." The captain checked his watch.

"Probably, sure." Max stared down at the floor, clicking his heels together in contemplation.

"Well, maybe she could teach you a thing or two?"

"Okay, sir. Okay! I get it! I'll be backstage." Max started toward the stairwell.

"Good. Oh, here. Take these to get started!" The captain handed him a stack of scripts for introductions, speeches, and port presentations. "Remember to stay on script. Just read the teleprompter."

Dim hues of black lights lined the corridor to the vacant dressing room. Illuminating a narrow path wedged between set designs, curtains, and low-hanging spotlights, the welcoming gleam of a vanity drew Max closer. Sifting through the thick volume of prose, he slipped into a wicker chair and unsheathed a red pen.

How many recitals has this man logged? He blew dust off the leather cover. "This isn't a manual," he whispered into the mirror, flipping through the first few pages to the table of contents. "It's a survival guide."

Hundreds of pages outlined every comment, complaint, and possible scenario that may arise onboard and ashore.

1. *Checklist*
2. *Team Breakdown*
3. *Life at Sea*
4. *Emergency Procedures*
5. *Handover Notes*

Handover? What's that about? Max flipped to the end and read: *In the event of my death, herein lies the blueprint to govern M.S. World One. Death? Did he ever plan to step down?* Max investigated, consumed by the text as he leaned-in for a closer look.

"Hellooo!" Ella rushed in.

"Ahh!" Max jumped, slamming the book shut and pushing it aside.

"Whatcha doing back here?" she prodded, trying to catch a glimpse of the manual.

"Quite the entrance! Are you trying to give me a heart attack?" Max slid the book behind his back in a feeble attempt to conceal it.

"Well, yeah. of course! Did it work?" She sat on the vanity in front of him, overtaking his whole station.

"You're subtle. Has anyone told you that before?" He smirked, forfeiting all desire to study.

"You and your books." She snatched a copy from behind him. "This one's as old as the captain. Oh, wait. It *is* his!" She flipped through the contents.

"Sometimes it's important to hold on to old things." Max grappled with her to give it back. "Old books can stand the test of time, with their lessons resonating throughout the ages. Who are we? To not have the humility to learn from generations of—"

"Booring!" Ella blurted out, pretending to fall asleep before stealing the book back and making a run for the stage.

"Boring?!" He chased after her, stumbling over cables, amplifiers, and costumes before breaching the curtain.

"Yeah! Boring!" she teased, running around the stage with the book before throwing it into the empty grandstands.

"Hey! What'd you do that for!" He slid off the front to retrieve it.

"Don't be stupid, Max. No one is going to listen to you if you stand up here reading a stuffy script!" She danced around a microphone stand, sliding it effortlessly across the stage in front of him, just in time for his return. "Lights, please!" She clapped, signaling the production booth.

This is the most dramatic woman I've ever met! "Ugh, wait a second. I just need to review these lines and find my glasses, and—"

"Action!" Ella shouted, cuing the music.

Words appeared and retreated from a trio of teleprompters outlining the arena. Their dated cursive font sped past his oration like a tsunami of prose, rattling the amphitheater with broken sentences until a porthole window cracked from interference.

Curious bystanders crowded near the reception marquee to witness the train wreck, attracting the unwanted attention of suspicious officers.

"Congratulations!" Ella applauded. "That's the worst performance of your career!" she shouted before disappearing behind the curtain.

SPLITTING SHIPS

Days turned to weeks as *M.S World One* sailed south toward the equator. The gentle rocking of swells against the hull turned into patterned repetitions as it became impossible to discern where one day ended and the next began. Tinkering with a broken record player in an abandoned lounge, Max counted the skipping needle as an approaching coastline came into view through a porthole.

Finally, land! He scurried up to the observation deck to find Ella watering their garden. The extended reposition enriched their kindling romance. Spending days walking the same promenade, climbing the same stairwells, and admiring the same artwork. Close quarters tended to bring out the best, or worst, in seafarers. Glancing down at couples embracing on their balcony verandas, or throwing their luggage overboard in agitation, Max was glad that their confinement ushered in a greater sense of intimacy. *How did I get so lucky?* He counted his blessings, stroking her hair in admiration.

"I need to get ready for rehearsal. Are you going to be alright up here?" She idled softly against the railing without waiting for a response. "Don't cut back the roses too far; they might not come back next bloom." She plucked a flower from its stem and kissed him goodbye before sliding down the stairs and out of sight.

Focusing back on their garden, Max basked in the beauty of their creation. *I think I'll just let these grow.* He tossed aside a pair of clippers to follow her down the stairs for a walk around the promenade deck.

An eerie ambiance radiated around the ship as packs of passengers paced the halls. Separate clusters of passengers donned blue or orange uniforms and explored every lounge, corridor, and breakout venue as they prepared for their delayed disembarkation. *Why does everyone look like stowaways? Have we really been at sea this long?* Max glanced in the windows as he strolled the promenade.

"Hey, Max! Lovely weather today, isn't it?" a passenger greeted him, his dark blue cardigan blending into the freshly painted hull.

"Move it, jerk!" another demanded, her burnt-orange sport coat blowing in the wind as she whisked past him.

"Great show the other day!" Another waved, his teal frames protecting inspired eyes. "I've planned a hike excursion for our next port!"

"Get out of the way, punk!" A runner clipped Max's shoulder in a flash of orange aggression, spitting in his direction.

What's with the divide? Max was caught off guard by the mixed encounters.

Rounding the teak deck for a final lap, the muffled sound of Henk's voice echoed within a nearby corridor. *He sounds distraught.* Max went inside the hull, following the sound through a maze of lounges and conference rooms before reaching its source within the notorious Pinnacle Pub. Its ominous satin curtains shielded a haze of smoke from polluting the spotless reception atrium below.

Holding his breath, Max tiptoed inside.

"Who do you think you are, one of us? Or one of them? Pick one!" Price reprimanded, circling Henk's beaten figure like a shark as two striped officers tied him to a chair within the pub.

"It's not that easy, Price." Henk pleaded.

Lurking in the smokey rafters above, Max dodged a roaming spotlight to narrowly evade detection.

"Yes. It is that easy," Price screamed in Henk's face with bloodshot eyes. "What's the count?" he ordered, barking at his henchmen for a status report.

"It's 50/50, but slightly more blue than orange pacing the promenade today."

"That's not good enough. Must be that stupid kid. Max! Where is he? Bring him to me!" Price declared, commencing the manhunt as a platoon dispatched their search.

"I'll give you one last chance, Henk. Are you one of us or one of them?" Price prodded, tapping a pair of scissors on Henk's shoulder, threatening to strip him of his rank and cut off his stripes. Watching from the shadows, Max held his breath, debating whether and when to intervene.

"You know, Price. There's one thing that trumps all orders, something intangible, something… real." Henk mustered the courage to continue despite the certainty of yet another beating. "It's that which has no rank but possesses authority over all."

"Oh, yeah? Are *you* trying to lecture *me*, boy? You should really learn to respect your elders!" Price punched Henk across the face, fracturing his jaw.

Slumped over in his chair, Henk struggled to regain his composure. Glancing toward the ceiling to prevent a bloody nose, Max revealed himself, silently applauding Henk's resolve as the two locked eyes.

Max scanned the space, marking scattered furniture and loose sound equipment for a timely ambush.

"There's only one thing I respect, sir, and it's certainly not you," Henk continued, laboring through his wounds.

"Oh, yeah? What's that?" Price scoffed, winding up for a finishing blow.

"The truth!" Max yelled down from the rafters, hurling a barstool onto Price, knocking him on his back as he slid down a rope to untie Henk.

"Throw them in the brig!" Price retaliated, pressing his pocket-watch to signal reinforcements. In a matter of seconds, dozens of officers donning orange coats flooded the pub.

A storm of debris flew across the room as the bar fight escalated into a gladiator match. Realizing they were outnumbered, Henk and Max assembled a bunker at the apex of the triangular lounge. More smoke filled the air. An officer threw another barstool at the two dissenters. Wood imploded into splinters near Max's face as he shielded his eyes.

Suddenly, a voice cut through the chaos. "Quickly! They won't be able to hold them off much longer!"

Max peered above their makeshift bunker to see a militia of passengers draped in blue lifejackets joining the fray.

Peering over their bunker, Max surveyed the battlefield. An ocean of blue and orange passengers collided with the standing guard of striped officers.

"Come on, Henk. We can't just sit here! Grab that cable!" Max ordered, gripping one end of an audio cord as the pair clothes-lined an orange platoon. Blow for blow, they pummeled each other with anything they could crack, shatter, and sharpen as the fight raged on for hours.

As their endurance staggered, wounded and unconscious bodies lay resting in between the two sides of the space, their division becoming more prominent as their colors drifted further and further apart. *What's that famous saying? A ship divided against itself… cannot float?* Max paused, resting underneath the bar for cover as he strategized a way to end the civil war.

"Attention, everyone, this is your Captain speaking." One long piercing wail triggered the emergency alarm as everyone covered their ears in discomfort. "This is not a drill, I repeat, this is not a drill. We have hit the peak of an underwater ridge on our final approach to Cartagena. Muster at your assigned assembly stations immediately."

Great. I knew this was trouble. Max staggered to his feet, dodging microphones and drumsticks hurling through the air and smashing against the walls behind him. "Come on, Henk, we need to make a run for it!"

Unholstering a CO_2 extinguisher from the wall beside them, Henk popped the pin and cleared a path through the combat.

"No. No. No! Not that way! Our muster station is up here!" Henk ushered Max toward the promenade.

I can't leave without Ella. "Go on without me! I'll be right there!" Max shouted, tripping over a cracking corridor as it began splitting the ship in half.

"Ella! Ella, we need to leave, now!" He searched, frantically opening the dressing room doors backstage to find her.

Where is she? He donned a nearby lifejacket to check his muster station. *Maybe she's already on the boat deck?*

As he darted up the grandstands to Roulette Stage, the entire auditorium split in half, rattling the steel hull below as water rushed into the theatre. Flocks of passengers panicked as they stumbled up the steps, desperately trying to escape the rushing water below, some shrieking in terror as they fell to their doom from the splintered balconies above.

"Max! Max! Come quickly!" Ella shouted from her muster station, unlatching the hooks connecting a lifeboat to its berth as it swung recklessly against the port-side railings. It blew violently with the wind, and her last hope of escape listed mercilessly with the ship as the hull cracked beyond repair.

I don't know if I'll make it in time. He sprinted down the boat deck, watching in terror as the separation began to widen, opening a trench of seafoam and debris in the water below.

"It's too wide! I won't make it!" he shouted back as the sound of warped steel along a fractured keel finally thundered into a traumatic split as the ship broke completely in half. Still afloat, two identical structures of a once magnificent whole slowly drifted apart with each approaching swell. The jagged tear along its former keel resembled a menacing peak of submerged ocean ridges, aloof to the devastation and horror that transpired in their wake.

"Here, grab this!" Ella tossed a life ring down from the observation deck across the gap, landing precisely around his body, immobilizing him in place.

"Will you wait for me?!" she shouted as tears ran down her cheeks onto her torn jumper.

"Yes!" he shouted, helplessly watching the tango of fractured hulls drift farther and farther apart. Still miraculously afloat, their warped skeletons waded with the tide. Carrying with them the embers of a civil war across hemispheres, still yet to be extinguished.

ETERNAL EXPEDITIONS

All seemed to be lost as half of the remains of *M.S. World One* drifted carelessly into the Port of Cartagena. Debris floated between anchored cargo ships as the tired hunk of steel maneuvered through a crowded harbor. Rising and falling with the tide, it finally waded into a dry-dock berth to commence its lengthy repair.

"What the hell happened down there?" Captain Lex fumed, pulling Max out from under the wreckage.

"It was an ambush, sir. A civil war! Price was planning a coup." Max dusted himself off, nursing a limp as he cast off a mooring line to connect with the pier.

"Well, a lot of good that did us! There's not much left to salvage, let alone command." The captain helped pull the rope tight, fastening it to the anchor chain before letting down the gangway into the terminal. "Better make yourself comfortable here, boy. It'll be a while until we're ready to set sail again. How's your Spanish?"

Max slumped, limping down the gangway and off into the streets of Old Town, Cartagena.

The subtle sound of espresso machines and coffee grinders whisked through the air.

What's that smell? Max trailed the aroma down rainbow-splashed streets of cobblestone and clay.

"Hey, watch it!" A local fruit vendor cycled past, narrowly missing trampling his feet. *Maybe next time, I'll be lucky enough to get hit.* His depressed slouch barely motored a shuffled stride. Glancing over his shoulder, the wreckage of *M.S. World One* floated ashore as a village of mechanics started their repairs.

"Why the stiff stride, *amigo*?" A coffee barista ushered him into the shop.

Where do I start? He sulked over to the entrance. *"Hola, uno Americano por favor?"*

"Si, mucho gusto," he confirmed, sensing an aura of heartbreak and destitution. "This one's on the house."

"Gracias, señor." Max took a long sip of the fresh brew, dripped overnight through a Yama tower. *Whoa! That's a jolt to the chest.* He perked up, venturing a wandering eye around the mosaic-tiled floor and continental map of South America plastered behind the serving counter. *Quite the operation. How much of the world imports coffee from here?*

Max eavesdropped on a local merchant. "No, no, no. I told you to put the horse *in front of* the cart. The cart doesn't pull the horse, *now does it?* How do you expect to get these beans loaded and shipped by the weekend with that kind of thinking?"

What now? The conversation drew nearer, finally breaching the coffee shop archway.

"What will it take to move that kind of volume through port? We don't have time for this. I'm no farmer, but these beans look tired and pathetic. Kinda like that bloke!" A tan figure draping a leather satchel pointed to him with disdain.

Who's this pompous jerk? Max squeezed his fists, priming for a fight. "Hey, watch your tone!"

"Oh, it has a pulse?" The man paced around the shop, his polished boots blending grit with showmanship as they clacked across the tile floor. His ripped jeans and tainted leather belt told the tales of a thousand scuffles as the tattoo of a raven pierced through the sleeves of his ragged black tank top.

"*De donde eres?* You're a bit far from home, *amigo*. Better watch your tongue." Detecting Max's accent, he glared over the brim of a double espresso from the far side of the bar, eyes bloodshot from the caffeine adrenaline.

I know that twang. What's a Norwegian doing in South America? "Probably not far from your neck of the woods, brother." Max slid a stool toward his perch to diffuse the tension.

"You're a Jersey boy, aren't ya?" He sat, slamming his mug on the counter. "Can't go a day without your *coffee* fix, huh? What brings you south of the border?"

Is it that obvious? Damn. "South! South Jersey, thank you," Max defended. "Shipwrecked, unfortunately. We hit the ridge."

"Ah, so it's your ship in dry dock," the stranger mused. "Figured. Your face says it all. Looks like you're in a rut, kid." He slid his stool closer.

Who does this guy think he is? I'm wasting my time. Max stood to pay the bill, dusting off his jacket in defiance as he turned to leave.

"Who's the girl?"

Max froze. "Does it matter? What's it to you?" He squinted, brows raised in suspicion.

"Let's just say I've been around the horn a few times." The man slicked back his long brown hair as he pointed to Cape Horn on the wall map behind the counter. "Name's Tio."

Tio? Sounds like a stage name. "Okay, Tio, I'll bite. Name's Max." They shook hands as he sat back down, studying the continental outline and nautical passages defining the Patagonian peninsula.

"Okay, Max. Let me set the hook then." Tio smirked at his naive facade. "Based on that feeble quiver in your step, your girl didn't make the split, did she?" Tio clutched a locket strung around his neck.

"Alright what's your angle?" Max cut the small talk.

"Hmmm. Perfect. We have much to discuss, in too short of time. I need a recruit to help me circumnavigate the continent in a cargo exchange. Seeing as you're marooned until the repairs are finished, how about an excursion?" Tio waved to the barista for a double shot of espresso.

"What's in it for me?" Max pressed. *If this guy has any more caffeine,* he might just erupt.

"We can't rush the clock, kid. You're stuck here, regardless, but it sure beats the boondocks, hostels, and brothels. Plus, you may just learn a thing or two." Tio dangled an old pocket-watch with a bright blue hue from his satchel.

Cargo exchange? Sounds more like pirating but he has a point. "Alright, I'm in. What's the itinerary?" Max unsheathed his watch and slammed it on the bar next to Tio's, both dials heading 9 o'clock, west toward Manta, Ecuador.

"We have our heading! Meet on the pier at sunset." Tio took another shot of espresso before throwing the mug at the map on the wall in dramatic departure. Instead of shattering to pieces, the wall absorbed the mug, illuminating a dotted course along the perimeter of the continent.

"Come on, come on, *rapido*, faster!" Tio mushed a caravan of loading crew across the gangway as they loaded the final bags of coffee into steerage.

Is this a ship or a floating antique? Max debated, pacing the rickety boards on the topside deck.

"We'll take it from here, gents. *Adios!*" Tio praised them, cutting their checks and bidding them farewell as Max untied the mooring lines.

What's with the hourglass downtown? Is that filled with coffee beans? Turning to Tio at the helm, Max yelled, "Hey! What's the deal with the town center? Why is everyone congregating around that hourglass?"

"This country runs on coffee, mate. The people worship it. A shame really. Not many Northerners get to witness the ritual," Tio explained, casting off from the pier and toward the open ocean.

Ritual? Northerners? This guy's out of his mind. Uncovering a periscope to peer out behind the wake, he saw the entire village gathered around the city center, collectively flipping the hourglass as the final bean dropped to the bottom vase—signaling an end to the day's production.

"I'll take the first shift," Tio volunteered, gripping the helm as the pair ventured farther and farther west. "Best get your rest. We'll need a fresh start for our arrival to Manta in the morning." He gripped the locket tight around his neck again in remembrance.

Curious, yet reserved. Max hobbled down the creaking hallway to a hammock strung up above a sack of beans. *I wonder what's in that locket?* He drifted off into a deep slumber.

Minutes turned to hours as their vessel steered toward the Ecuadorian coast. The subtle swirl of a land-breeze hardly diffused the humidity as the pair sweat through their cotton shirts and worn denim. Ripping his jeans into shorts, Max fastened the residual fabric into a net and cast it overboard. It trolled the passing wake for a matter of seconds until it snagged a yellowfin tuna.

"Got one!" he called out to Tio, reeling in their breakfast knot-by-knot until the fish splashed onto the top-deck. Filleting it on the spot, he recycled the remains into the harbor as they approached the dock. *Whoa! Look at all of them!* Max pointed in awe, watching hundreds of fish breaching the water in a seemingly limitless supply.

"Yeah, yeah, I remember my first catch," Tio scoffed, unimpressed by the feat. "Like shootin' fish in a barrel over in these waters, kid!" He shook his head at Max's virgin amusement.

Welcome to Manta, Fishing Capital of the South, read an arched sign, etched in fish bones.

"First stop. Let's see how much we can trade. Grab three of those bags, will ya?" Tio motioned toward the coffee, pulling Max ashore by the shirt collar as they dragged their heap to market.

The beaches winded like an old snake, flaring into the streets like flaking scales on a tired skeleton. *How long have these huts been used?* Max cringed, inspecting their battered frames and gut-stained cutting boards with a queasy stomach as fishermen cleaned their catch. Hundreds of seagulls loitered on the shingled roofs, squawking in unison as splattered slices of meat pinged their attention.

"Stay here. Don't draw any attention," Tio whispered, hoisting the bags over his shoulder as he disappeared into the market.

What does he think I'll do? A juggling act? Magic show? Shaking his head in defiance, Max leaned passively against an empty fishing net hanging from the rafters.

A ship's horn sounded from a nearby pier as it came alongside their cargo. *That's odd. What's all the commotion?* Max witnessed a coast guard raid from afar. Swarms of orange zodiacs surrounded a clunky iron fishing vessel like a ravenous flock of seagulls, ushering away a crew of foreign charter fishermen in handcuffs.

I need to warn Tio. Max yanked away from the fishing net, tripping in its wrappings as he stumbled into the market. *We better make sure this exchange is clean...*

"What do you mean *only two* tons of tuna? Don't you sell by capacity? My rig can store at least twenty!" a familiar raspy voice bartered.

"Any more than two, and it'll expire before you round the horn!" a feminine voice lectured.

"So, you don't want my money, is what you're saying?"

"If we sold our catch to more of you lot, we'd all starve," she reprimanded, throwing a handful of coffee beans into Tio's face as Max reached the booth. "Who's this? Your apprentice? Ha! Good luck, kid," she greeted from behind the counter.

Pulling Tio aside, Max whispered, "We have company. Merchant marine charter vessel. Local police arrested the crew."

"Fine. Let's move." Tio swiftly ended the negotiation by settling for two tons. "Have your boats meet us alongside the pier in an hour. Not a minute longer." He gestured toward the woman as they fled the market.

Reaching a barricade to their dock, Tio said, "What's going on here? Officers? Hello? Tio waved down a patrol. Yeah, you. That's my ship!" He pointed to their cargo slip adjacent to the raid.

"ID?" an officer asked.

The pair reluctantly surrendered their passports and waited for clearance as the patrolman scanned an international database, validating their credentials. "You're clear but hurry it up. We're restricting the area."

"What's going on?" Max asked, observing hundreds of tons of tuna being unloaded and confiscated from the neighboring vessel.

"Illegal fishing. The charter's over capacity. Isn't the first time we've needed to raid in these waters." The patrolman shrugged. "At least ten years' jail time," he continued, sensing a nervous jitter from Tio as they passed through the barricade and up the gangway to their ship.

"*Hasta Luego!*" Tio belted at the platoon as they cast off from the dock. "Max, rudder to starboard." He steered toward a pier opposite the harbor.

Cranes began loading fish into steerage as forklifts transferred bags of coffee ashore. *Seems like a fair trade. Two thousand fish for enough coffee to keep the fishermen awake for a year straight.* Max paced the top-deck, studying the whole operation intently.

"Okay, here's the last of it," the woman from the market confirmed, releasing a final net of tuna fillets as they slid into the last container. "You'll need to stop in Lima and Punta Arenas on your way to keep them from spoiling." She glared, hands throttling a police radio as an implied threat.

"Pleasure." Tio saluted sarcastically, eager to venture further south.

"Oh, and one more thing…" She paused, waving forward a young woman donning deep-sea coveralls and a highlighter yellow lifejacket. The only feature distracting from her bleach-blond hair and red lipstick was her stark demeanor as she clambered aboard, wielding a titanium set of chef knives.

"Who the hell is this?" Tio questioned, crossing his arms in protest.

"My daughter, Esmeralda. Ezz for short. She'll keep an eye on the inventory for you," the woman said, bidding her farewell.

"Great. A heartbroken stowaway and now, a dicey babysitter. What am I, a privateer or a babysitter?" Tio grunted, starting the engines and making a heading for the Peruvian coast.

Ignoring Tio's grudge, Max slid down a railing into the cargo hull and offered to help her unpack.

"Why, thank you, *muchas gracias*." Esmerelda washed away her first impression with a cheeky smile, delighted to make his acquaintance.

"Are you a chef?" Max inferred as she packed away a white coat and frying pan from her rucksack.

"Congratulations, Captain Obvious," she teased, unlatching her lifejacket and stowing it beneath the bottom bunk. "Come on, let's keep an eye on that greedy scoundrel." She shooed Max out of her cabin before slamming the door behind them.

"Land, ho!" Tio announced, tossing the wheel back and forth in a delirious juggling act. *He's been up there all night.* Max sympathized, prepping a platter of tuna for Ezz to sauté.

"Alright, y'all, let's make this a quick turnaround. We need to keep a tight schedule. You!" Tio motioned to Max. "Keep a close eye on that one," he warned, scowling at Ezz. "Mira Flores is full of delicates. No need to buy everything you see."

Paragliders leaped from steep cliffs as street performers hustled around a bustling shopping center in downtown Lima. Luxury lines showcasing the finest alpaca cotton west of the Andes tempted Ezz and Max as they swerved through the crowded walkways in search of a suitable exchange for their Columbian stash.

"Socks, neckties, mittens, shirts, parkas. What's with this llama obsession?" Max chuckled.

"I don't know, but if you ask me, it's all overpriced bull—" Ezz began.

"Whoa! Look at this!" Max pointed out, holding a knit suit jacket and collarless dress shirt. "Feel this fabric!" he continued, rubbing the sleeve up against his cheek.

"No need to swaddle it," Ezz replied, rolling her eyes. "Weren't you supposed to be watching out for me?" she mocked, catching a glimpse of copper cookware. "Wait a minute. Let's pick up a few of these!" She stopped in front of a full kitchen set.

"No, no, no. We can't afford it! How many bags of coffee is that worth? Plus, we'll never get back to Cartagena at this rate. Hurry up," Max lectured.

Minutes turned into hours as the pair window shopped the strips in Mira Flores, finally returning to the dock with armfuls of clothes, pots, pans, and a special gift for Tio.

"Where have you been? Do you realize what time it is?" Tio yelled, furious with their tardiness as the sun began to set beyond the cliffs.

"Well, we may have gotten carried away," the pair uttered, slightly embarrassed by their lack of restraint as they climbed back aboard.

"Here." Ezz threw a winter coat at his feet. "You're going to need it," she warned, double-checking a voyage chart portraying the jagged teeth of Cape Horn looming ahead of them.

LIMITLESS ADVENTURE

———

Wind swirled relentlessly around the bow of the ship as it drifted into the Strait of Magellan, winding back and forth through a maze of sandbars hidden beneath the shallow waters flooding the Chilean Fjords. Shedding hundreds of tons of coffee in Mira Flores, the empty cruiser felt more like an expedition clipper than a cargo barge. With most of their fortune converted from beans to pesos, they finally had enough cash to chart a course back to Cartagena and fund the repairs for *M.S. World One.*

"Hard on port!" Max navigated from the railing, signaling a steep bend in the channel ahead.

"Watch it!" Ezz shouted from the cargo hull, fumbling a frying pan as cutlery shifted with the dramatic bank.

"Okay, okay! I hear you," Tio barked, gripping the wheel level.

Fjords converged at the southernmost tip of the Chilean peninsula, creating a temperature vortex as they approached the last cluster of civilization marking the end of the world. Its rugged terrain crumbled with crosswinds racing across the Pacific before crashing into the continental ridge defining the Andes mountains. Fishing shacks and lighthouses lined the rocky coast, each with a lantern warning sailors of looming shipwrecks as citizens scurried home before nightfall.

A familiar raven flew overhead. *What now?* A strong gust of wind rattled the hull, swaying the ship dangerously close to Cape Horn's perilous jaws.

"Brace yourselves!" Tio shouted from the helm, helplessly clinging to a mast as the ship came within striking distance of the rocks. At the very last moment, another gust nudged them back into the trade winds, narrowly avoiding a collision as flaking cedar shingles scraped away from the battered hull.

"What are you doing up there?" Ezz shouted in contempt. "Are you trying to get us all killed?"

"I'd like to see you give it a go!" Tio challenged, straining to be heard over a rising thunder of wind.

Will these two ever get along? Max fought back the wind as it anchored him in place, forced to silently observe their pointless scuffle.

"Give me that!" Ezz demanded, finally reaching the helm as the ship took another sharp turn, back toward the rocks.

"Careful what you wish for." Tio smirked, releasing his grip on the wheel.

"Come on, not that way," Ezz gasped, fighting the wind with all her strength.

Tio gripped the wheel, attempting to support her. "Pull!" he shouted, desperately trying to veer away from the cliffs.

Another strong gust pushed them farther away from the coast, just before impact.

"What's the point?" Ezz vented, exhaling a sigh of relief. "Does it even matter if we steer or not?"

"Absolutely!" Tio affirmed, voice cracking from the shallow lie. "You think this clipper can round the horn without me?"

"Hands off the helm," Max intervened, pressing himself between them with two extended stiff-arms.

"What did you say, boy?" Tio replied.

"We'll get where we need to go." Max sensed the danger ahead and how poorly equipped the team was to handle it.

"You don't know what you're doing, kid!" Tio grumbled as they picked up speed. "We're going the wrong way!" He gripped the helm harder, fighting the crosswind.

"Max! What's the deal?" Ezz prodded. "We can't just let the ship steer itself! Are you mad?" She pulled harder, shoving Tio aside to reinforce their aggressive heading.

"Well, it's better than listening to you two bicker over who's in charge!" he lectured, pointing a shaky finger in their faces.

Suddenly, the helm broke off from its mount. Wooden handles lay scattered in a pile of scrap on the topside deck, splintered from the struggle.

"Great! Damn thing can't handle it!" Tio muttered, flicking the battered pieces overboard as they floated away toward the coast.

"Well, if you would have just let me have a try," Ezz scowled.

"We'll get where we need to go," Max repeated, stepping in between them as the clipper sprinted farther south.

Icebergs began to appear alongside steep caverns in approaching channels as their ship self-navigated through the Antarctic landscape. An eerie silence, broken only by the subtle squawking of distant penguin colonies, encompassed a surreal void of snow-capped mountains and motionless ice shelves, preserved in an eternal slumber.

Staring at each other in a hypnotic state of reverie, the trio sat speechless, admiring the quiet stillness as they ventured deeper into the continent.

Why is that so special? Max glanced over at Tio clutching the locket around his neck, afraid to inquire further.

Peering over the railing, he gazed into a nearby glacier. *Where's Ella?* He felt guilty for their prolonged separation. Even after all this time apart, he still felt her presence idling beside him.

Visions shifted into a mirage as premonitions of loss and longing flooded his imagination. *Is their ship repaired? Did they even make it across the Atlantic?* Despite floating through the most majestic place on the planet, he couldn't stop thinking about her.

A raven swooped down over a nearby ridge, landing on the railing next to him. Its talons clutched a glass bottle containing a blank piece of parchment and a quill. Feeling the sudden urge to send her a message, Max retrieved the bottle, unraveled the scroll, and began to write:

> *Embarked on a cargo expedition to earn enough*
> *money for the ship repair. Captain's a bit...*
> *well...jaded.*
> *Castaway to the bottom, or top, of the world.*
> *To the place where life begins and ends.*
> *Silent giants frozen in frame.*
> *Thawing to cleanse all that remains.*
> *Solitude becomes the fortress, beneath shades*
> *of blue.*
> *Patiently drifting between the wakes, of me and you.*

Signing his name with the ship's coordinates, *83° S, 135° E*, he rolled up the parchment and placed it back within the glass. "Make sure this gets to her," he whispered to the raven, returning the bottle to its talons before takeoff.

"Are you quite finished over there?" Tio blurted out, emerging from his defeated slump. "Are we just going to sit here and stare at each other, or are we going to think of a way out of this godforsaken wasteland?"

"Let him alone, Tio." Ezz searched a nearby trunk for an icepick and paddle to navigate the approaching cavern. "And it's not a wasteland. It's beautiful!" She paused for a moment to bask in the afternoon sun.

"Beautiful? We're stuck in the coldest, windiest, driest, widest, most desolate, useless, penguin-infested—"

"—most important place in the world," Max finished, patting Tio's shoulder.

"Well, *we* need an exit strategy," Tio fussed, shaking off Max's hand as he stomped toward the bow.

"Did you hear that, Ezz?" asked Max.

"Hear what?" she replied, mounting the paddle as a rudder.

"That's the first time Tio said *we*."

"Oh, don't expect much out of him. He'd pilot the ship himself if he could. Only reason we're here is to ensure he cashes his check back in Columbia." She shrugged, throwing Max the icepick to help navigate.

"Look! In the ice!" Tio shouted from the bow.

Frozen in a horseshoe channel, the outline of a mysterious object reflected with the waning sun inside a thin glacial wall ahead of them.

"Throw me the grapnel!" Tio ordered.

Rolling his eyes at Ezz, Max vaulted the heavy iron clamp of a nearby grapnel over Tio's stance, holding onto its rope as the hooks struck a glacial wall. It revealed a mystical conductor's baton encased in crystal quartz, reflecting lights from within the glacier walls.

"What the hell is this?" Tio grabbed hold of the rope and reeled it in. "Of all things to find, we get this flimsy little wand?"

"It's not flimsy if you use it correctly!" Ezz yelled, leaving her post to confront him.

"What do you want me to do with this stupid thing? Go whaling for a humpback to pull us north? It's not sharp enough to use as a hook let alone a spear!"

Here we go again, these two really need to work it out. Max grunted, taking control of the rudder.

"No, no, no! You're impossible to deal with!" Ezz threw a tantrum. "It's a conductor's baton. It doesn't work on its own!" She swiped it from his hands to demonstrate. "You use it to direct other people." She tapped it a few times and pointing it overhead. "I don't know how you survived this long without needing one unless you're just so self-absorbed that you haven't noticed!" she ridiculed, waving it back and forth methodically to illustrate her point.

Tio climbed down from the bow and took a seat beside Max, helping him steer. "Alright, Alright. Point taken."

Sound rippled across the valley of ice as a glacial wall collapsed, revealing the entrance to a cavern radiating a peculiar green light. Flashing on repeat like a honing beacon, it pulled their ship closer like a magnet as one final gust of wind pushed the vessel through the arched entranceway, transporting them to the docks of Buenos Aires, Argentina.

"*Buenos Dias, bienvenido a casa,*" the Harbor Master greeted them as he attached their mooring lines to the dock.

"What did he say?" Tio shuffled over to Max for translation.

"Good morning. Welcome home." Max rolled his eyes in embarrassment before vaulting over the railing and onto the pier. "Come on, Ezz. Let's get some fresh air, or should I say *fair winds*?"

"Don't mind me! I'll just stay here! We have a schedule to keep, remember!" Tio called after them. "Was it something I said?" he muttered under his breath.

Boards creaked beneath their feet as the pair explored the rustic marina. They dodged merchants, privateers, cargo pallets, and taxi drivers until they eventually came upon the art deco facade of a towering hotel. Tucked away from the traffic of the bustling port, its wrought iron doorway blended into the stone entrance like a living vine.

"Can we peek inside?" Ezz asked, pulling on Max's sleeve in quiet anticipation.

Noticing an elegant display beneath a gas lamp outside the entrance, they moved in for a closer look:

Tapas: Frio y Calor
Chorizo
Solomillo
Piquillo y Ceviche

"Max! Max! Do you know what this is?" Ezz jumped with excitement.

"A restaurant?" he asked, failing to see the significance.

"Not just a restaurant. This is a real tapas bar!" She shuffled forward, almost pressing her forehead to the display as she studied the menu.

"Yeah, so what? You can make anything you want back onboard." He leaned on the facade, holding back a laugh as she savored every last word on the specials list, salivating with anticipation.

"You mean anything with tuna," she denounced.

What's the big deal? I've never seen Ezz this excited.

"Table for two?" A welcoming hostess in a sleek black dress and leather heels stepped out from the foyer.

The room was dark. Very dark. The only things visible were flicking candles in the center of each table, illuminating circular marble high-tops. As they were seated, the floor between the tables rose to shoulder-height, creating a smooth labyrinth stage wrapping around the space as a waiter took their order.

"This is magnificent! A chef's dream." Ezz took a sip of white wine.

"Have you always loved cooking?" Max asked, intrigued by her passion for the culinary arts.

"I never really had the choice. Growing up in Ecuador, the world really relies on us to fish, and those fishermen… Well, not much room for a woman onboard."

"But you could have stowed away? Snuck aboard a charter vessel? You're probably better than most of them anyway."

"I couldn't leave my mother. My family. They would have been devastated." She took another swig. "Plus, they wouldn't have approved. 'The sea is no place for a woman,' they would say."

The waiter returned, carrying three platters of steak, chicken, and ceviche. Their sizzling aromas blended across the table, spreading delectable scents of paprika and oregano.

"What if you could cook anything you wanted? What would you choose?" Max asked, cutting a sliver of steak.

"It depends on where I am and who I'm with." She brushed aside the ceviche to construct a tower of chicken, seasoning it with mixed herbs before drizzling a dressing overtop in artful precision. "Cooking is much more than a profession; it's an art, like music or painting. It can be visual as much as tasteful."

"That's an interesting view on things."

"Ever since I was a little girl, I had to find an outlet, a way to detach from the mundane and the never-ending cycle of catch or release, clean and fillet. Cooking became my existence. My passion. My world."

Her face was barely visible above the candlelight between them, but Max sensed her fulfilment radiating from across the table. *This is where she's meant to be.*

Silverware chimed around them as dishes came and went from the kitchen. Minutes turned to hours as they dined, sharing adventures and memories of distant lands in almost pure darkness. The thought of returning to the docks to continue their voyage escaped their concern with each platter served.

Couples filled the seats around them as the evening grew later, warming the space with fond conversation and more delectable aromas. The subtle sound of an acoustic guitar resonated throughout the dining room, plucking to the rhythm of a percussionist as a curtain revealed the trio of Latin musicians.

A vocalist began reciting the first verse of a melancholic ballroom number as two dancers appeared draped in elegant sashes and shined leather shoes. The gentleman's slicked-back hair brushed a pressed collar beneath his chiseled jawline as he stared into the eyes of a determined partner. Her short, red dress waved side to side as she strutted toward center stage with focused precision. The band began a 2/4 rhythm as the duo began to tango. Their sharp, accented steps tapped the floor in passionate rudiments as they glided across the room, seemingly detached from the judgment around them.

"Beautiful." Ezz was fully immersed in the performance.

"We need to get going. We have a schedule to keep, remember?" Max insisted, breaking her trance.

"I can't. I've never felt so connected to a place in my life." Her face lit up with revelation as she admired the ambiance around her, eyes glazed in reverie as if finally experiencing a dream realized.

"But what about your family?" Max objected.

"This is where I'm meant to be, Max. Go on without me," she declared, seemingly strapped to her chair.

Conflicted by her decision and its almost certain consequences, Max raised his glass to bid her farewell. "To fair winds, and swift seas..."

"...and limitless adventure for all those who seek," she finished, toasting him goodbye as the soft rhythm of an electric guitar played him out as he disappeared beyond the gas-lamps.

Max retrieved the watch from his pocket and followed its heading back to the docks. *Tio's going to be furious.* Gazing up at the midnight sky, he admired the romantic aura of cobblestone and brick lining the boardwalk along the harbor on his way back to the docks. Its quiet elegance blended a harmonious splash of grit with passion. Rounding the last bend, his posture tensed, preparing to break the news of Ezz's immigration.

"What do you mean she's not coming?" Tio exploded. "Do you realize what this means?" He stomped across the topside deck in a tantrum.

"That she's happy? That she's finally making a decision for herself?" Max dodged the remainder of their fish, coffee, and an assortment of random objects within throwing distance of Tio.

"Who cares about her? What about me!" Tio slammed a bag of pesos onto a table next to a refurbished helm, beginning to count.

"Well, maybe, it's not always about you." Max joined him, drafting a balance sheet.

"I'll never be allowed back to Manta now. No, sir. Not me. If she wants to throw her life away to become some soppy, Tapas chef, fine. But don't take me down too." He stacked their last coin, realizing they were short of their target.

"Let's go, Max." Tio double-checked his watch before releasing the mooring lines and casting off.

Why can't he just be happy for her? Max paced back and forth as their ship retreated out of Rio de la Plata, turning north toward Brazil.

Exhausted from their extended journey around the continent, Max and Tio traded shifts at the tattered helm, unable to mark when one day ended and the next began. Determined to reach Cartagena in the coming days, but still short on funds for the repair and cargo exchange, they chartered an aggressive course, maxing out the speed of their empty clipper at thirty knots, parting with anything that bore extra weight, chairs, coffee bags, cutlery, pans, pots, extra bunks, and splintered cargo containers. Nothing was safe from disposal in their hellbent haste as their watches blinked in rapid succession, beaconing their swift return.

"One last stop; we're almost out of fuel," Tio croaked after several days of ruminating silence. "Maybe we can find a passenger to transport for a hefty price?"

Mist evaporated with the morning sunrise along the rolling peaks of dormant volcanoes as they sailed into the port of Rio de Janeiro.

Cutting it close, isn't he? Max slid down the cargo shaft to check the fuel gauge. "How long have we been on empty?" he shouted up from below deck.

Suddenly, the engine stopped chugging. Black smoke rose from the exhaust as the vessel coasted alongside a berth on Copacabana beach, barely connecting with the pier before a fire ignited the storage bay.

"Fire!" Max yelled, desperately unpinning an extinguisher to fight back the flames.

"Oh, you've got to be kidding me!" Tio clambered down the stairwell to join the battle.

"It's not working. I'm out of CO_2," Max gasped, squeezing the empty canister in disbelief as the flames grew stronger.

"Try the dry powder. Here." Tio tossed him another canister, just a little too late.

"Nothing, it's empty. We need to leave. Now!" Max conceded, throwing his effects into Ezz's rucksack before fleeing the scene.

"Damn it. Damn it! My ship!" Tio cried out in disbelief, tragically surrendering in anguish as he jumped overboard onto the beach.

Fire trucks and police vehicles stormed the pier, attaching wide hoses to nearby hydrants as they cleared the crowds assembling along Copacabana, watching in awe as their vessel burst into flames.

"Jesus Christ. Now what?" Tio lay motionless in the sand, his arm twisted behind his back like a wounded seagull as he nurtured badly burned legs in the shallow water, watching in horror as his livelihood burned to ashes.

"Well, we could just go ask him?" Max pointed toward the *Christ the Redeemer* statue on the summit of Corcovado, shouldering Tio's weight as he clambered to his feet.

Dodging blaring sirens and curious sunbathers, the pair navigated the exotic avenues of Ipanema en route to the base of the mountain.

Steaming with denial as he hobbled under Max's stride, Tio contemplated their options. "We both need to get back to Cartagena ASAP. With no ship, no money, and no friends in Brazil, our odds of making it back in time are slim."

There must be another way. Max rallied, pitying Tio as he limped toward an entrance hut marking the base of the trail.

Danger, Armed Thieves Operate in this Area, a sign warned, piked into the soil. Tracing the trek ahead, the steep, winding switchbacks seemed to wrap indefinitely around a jungle of poisonous vines and treacherous ditches along the 1.5-mile ascent.

"Empty your pockets," Max insisted, sifting through their effects. "Do we have anything worth stealing?"

A map, pair of sunglasses, water, extra shirts, socks, random journals, pens, parchment, and one watch blinking a bright blue hue encased in a leather sheath toppled out of the bag.

My watch! Where is it? Max patted his pockets in a frenzy. "Tio! I-I lost my watch! I won't be allowed to board without it!" He gasped, still rummaging around their rucksack, hoping to uncover its whereabouts.

"Have mine," Tio muttered, sensing his despair. "My time at sea is over," he said, finally accepting his fate as he hobbled over to a bench within the hut. "I can't make it, Max." He clutched the locket around his neck. "Here, I want you to have this too." He ripped it off to place it within Max's palm. Shedding a tear, he opened it one last time. The silhouette of a beautiful blonde woman in a woven ascot gazed back at him in heartbroken longing. Her hopeless eyes winked one last gesture of affection before vanishing from the frame, leaving the locket empty as Max closed the outer case.

"It's your time now, Max. Send a rescue team from the summit if you make it alive."

"I can't just leave you here!" Max insisted.

"It's too far. Go on without me."

Sensing Tio's stubborn pride, yet respecting his sense of urgency, Max packed up the rucksack and started his solo accent up Corcovado. Watch in hand, he traversed tropical switchbacks and dangerous pitfalls, winding back and forth around blind corners with a keen suspicion for thieves hiding in the brush the higher he climbed. Finally, after an hour and a half of steep bouldering, he reached the summit. Dripping with sweat, he collapsed to his knees in front of the towering soapstone sculpture stretching thirty meters into the sky.

I need a miracle, he pleaded to the statue, unlatching his rucksack as he caught his breath on the platform overlooking the glistening skyline of downtown Rio. The tropical peak of Sugarloaf protected the bustling marina as it taxied cable cars from the base to the summit.

Pacing back toward a lantern hitched to the side of the statue, he uncovered the outline of a music note engraved into the stone. *That's odd.* He hoisted the lantern above its weathered grooves. Raising a curious palm, he pressed the emblem into the pedestal beneath the statue, unlocking a secret entrance to a mystical dwelling.

"Hello?" he announced, keeping his body within the sunlit frame of the foyer. "Is anyone home?"

Time began to slow down. Literally. Not just time, but movement, thoughts, and reflections. Everything felt as though it crawled passively from one moment to the next. *This is torture.* He cringed, fumbling around for the light switch.

An Edison bulb illuminated the hollow shell as a record player spun slowly in the center of the room.

Another spotlight illuminated the frame of a man seated upright against the wall across the room. His dust-scorn face was slightly hidden under the brim of a wicker hat, but the cupped posture of his calloused palms and long fingers clearly cradled a vintage Stratocaster guitar.

"♩ ♩ ♫ ♪," he improvised, breaking into a slow blues.

"Yes. I'm in from out of town," Max replied, able to translate his riffs seamlessly.

"♫ ♫ ♫ ♫."

"What do you mean, I need to slow down?"

"♫ ♫ ♩ ♩."

"Okay, sure. Yes, I know what happens when you rush into things."

"♫ ♫ ♪ ♪."

"Well, what do you expect? You'd feel the same if you knew what Price is doing to these passengers and ports."

"♫ ♫ ♪ ♪."

"You used to work for Price? When? Where?"

"♩ ♩ ♩ ♩."

"So, you're aware of what's at stake?"

"♪ ♪ ♪."

"Yes, her name's Ella."

"♫ ♫ ♫ ♫."

"So now you understand. Yes, I should be rushing."

Awakening from his tonal trance, the figure rose from the floor. Unstrapping his guitar, he tipped his hat in acquaintance. "Seems I'm not the only musician on this rock anymore." he acknowledged, clearing the air as he holstered the Stratocaster.

"What's the fastest route to the Mediterranean?" Max pleaded.

"Always rushing, always chasing." The man shuffled carelessly across the foyer. "You'll need to be more patient if you're aiming to break up Price's Empire." He donned a featherweight fleece. "Name's Rez. As in *resilience.* My mother named me after the only thing she could muster before she died, not

that you'll spare the time to listen, let alone remember that."
He glanced at a portrait of a family on his mantel. "Come!
Let's take a walk. I'll explain more on the way."

Dusk shadowed a red sunset as the duo strolled deeper
into the mountaintop temple.

"Where are you from?" Max pried.

"New York City," Rez replied.

He couldn't drop that twang if he tried. "Oh, well, of
course! Who could deny it?" Max paced a step ahead.

"All this time away, and I still can't drop it. Seems that's
the last thing to go, aside from the suit." Rez smirked, slowing
his pace to keep Max on schedule. "It took me about a year or
two, but I eventually traded my $1000 pinstripe suit for a small
painting! I even cast my Rolex into the sea! It was freeing!"

Lanterns lined the cavern as the pair trekked farther
into the temple.

"You know, Max, I used to dine on Fifth Avenue and
Central Park every night back in the city," Rez continued.

"Every night? How did you manage to afford that?" Max
calculated, still pushing the pace.

"Well, I was an investment banker in my former life. You
know, assets, liabilities, trades, commissions, the works! I
wanted for nothing!" Rez daydreamed.

Max couldn't believe it. *Investment banking? That sounded
lucrative. How did a guy like that end up in a temple on a
mountaintop in South America?*

"That sounds expensive," Max replied. "What brings you
to Rio? Why did you give it all up?"

"Ah, see, that's what you're missing." Rez tipped his hat
lower with emphasis. "I had it all. The money, the penthouse
apartment, the flashy car, the corner office. Everything, that
is, everything with a price."

The pair finally reached the end of the cavern, revealing a flashing roulette wheel with a watch-shaped keyhole blinking a bright blue hue.

"You know, Max." Rez began strumming a guitar beside the wheel. "The more money I had, the more I earned, the more I needed to buy. It was a vicious cycle. So vicious that I found myself drowning in my own wealth." He scaled a minor pentatonic. "One day, I found myself buying friends, buying health, even buying women until I had enough. I just couldn't take it anymore, so I booked a bus ticket to Atlantic City."

This is getting ugly. I'm sorry I asked. Should I cut him off?

"Round and round and round, the roulette wheel spun. Finally, I placed a bet, wagering my net worth on black. Round and round and round, the roulette wheel spun. Finally, the ball dropped: Red. I was broke. So do you know what I did?" He continued strumming, louder and more distorted this time. "I climbed to the roof of the casino to end it all. My feet dangled over the edge of the tallest resort in that decrepit excuse for a city. But just as I leaned forward to take my last breath, a ship emerged along the horizon line. Its bright green light radiated like a beacon from heaven."

Max gasped, trying to keep a steady beat. "But wait, Rez. Didn't you work for Price? Couldn't he have helped you get back on your feet?"

"Of course, half the city did, when he first came back to Atlantic City, sailing into the marina in a grand display of pomp and circumstance. It was the most grandiose homecoming I've ever seen. Flags hoisted his name on every pole and wrapped around every super yacht anchored in the back bay. He was welcomed in like a hero returning from battle, promising wealth and new beginnings to everyone in his wake."

"But what happened? Last I heard, his casino is set for demolition."

"Turns out he never paid our salaries. Every time we 'passed go' and backed another construction contract, he would rob the community chest to make the payments. It wasn't until the whole town exiled him that he gave up his property and declared bankruptcy. Amazing, really, how everyone joined forces to flush him out to sea like that."

Continuing a melancholy strum, he shifted to the major pentatonic. "So, Max, in my last moments atop that towering gallows overlooking the ocean, I realized the most important thing about life. The one thing that money can't buy. The one thing that doesn't have a price."

"What's that?" Max leaned in, subconsciously gripping Tio's locket.

"I think you've already found it."

Holstering his guitar, Rez extended his hands for Max's watch. Still gripping the locket around his neck, Max delivered it as the roulette wheel began flashing faster, revealing a portal back to Cartagena. Winding its gears to set the right pace, Rez placed Max's watch on the keyhole and pulled the slot lever, beginning the final spin to transport him back to *M.S. World One.*

"But wait, Rez! How will we repair the ship? We can't afford it!" Max yelled over the spinning wheel as its lever snapped back into place.

"Speak to the maidenhead, for only she can unlock the lessons of the past."

Retrieving his watch from the slot machine, Max held his breath and walked through the roulette wheel. Clutching Tio's locket, he walked in blind faith toward his destiny beaconing beyond the frame.

A CITY IN THE SAND

"Meet me where our days begin and end, over the line where time stops ticking," a ghostly voice called to Max as he reappeared on the docks of Cartagena. "*Max*," it called again. He felt his whole-body tingle with paranormal possession as he glided across the pier, being drawn closer and closer to the fractured hull of *M.S. World One.*

"Who's there? What do you want from me?" Max shouted into the morning mist blanketing the port.

"Embark on a voyage less traveled," the ghostly voice whispered again through the fog as the gangway revealed an entrance to the atrium, its gas lanterns illuminating a treasure map dotting the teak decks along the promenade.

Step by step, Max followed their trail, climbing over abandoned lounges, thrown cabins, and broken glass from the shipwreck. "Meet me where our days begin and end," the voice whispered from a nearby corridor.

Where our days begin and end? Where time stops ticking? Max riddled. *Atlantis Hall!*

Sprinting toward the aft of the ship, Max threw open what was left of the entrance doors. Their shattered glass crunched beneath his feet as he made haste toward the pearl-encrusted grandfather clock within the dining room. Stride for stride, he leaped across the evaporating staircase up to the third floor, following the ghostly voice as it grew louder with every step.

"Where are you? Show yourself!" Max demanded.

"A ship without its maiden is a lost soul at sea." The voice echoed around the chamber, reverberating off abandoned silverware and wine flutes. "Best not lose your head." A sharp chef knife darted across the room, narrowly missing Max's neck as it stabbed into the back of the grandfather clock.

Troubled, yet more curious than afraid, Max answered, "Who are you?"

Floating out of the pearl pendulum beneath the clock-tower, a woman in white glided toward him. Struck with fascination, not fear, Max mirrored her gaze. Hypnotized with reverie, he reached out his hand to touch hers, attempting to lock fingers in a transcendent embrace as if blending the glory of the past with the promise of a brighter future.

"Good evening, Mr. Shades." The woman wore a 1920s-era evening gown and white gloves. A string of pearls dangled from her neck as she adjusted a flashy crown atop her head while a white sash with gold lettering revealed her royal appointment, *Margaret Gorman, the original Ms. America.*

"A curse has been laid upon this vessel. A ship divided against itself surely cannot sail. Yet be forewarned that an eternity of destitution lay upon this hunk of steel unless properly christened and governed by its rightful godmother. Will you be the one to bring harmony to the seas? To rebuild a city in the sand, forged by your own shovels, crafted by your own hands?"

What is this lady talking about? Godmothers? Sandcastles? "Listen, Ms. America. If you think I can build a city alone then you're definitely a mirage of my imagination. But what's this about godmothers?"

She glided onto the teak floor, becoming more realistic with each passing moment. Unsheathing a golden watch-key from beneath the clock, she began to turn back time. Round and round she spun the clock, winding it back to the summer of 1921, the date of her coronation. Suddenly, the façade of the room changed. Broken glass repaired itself, tablecloths were stripped and chairs were full of seated mariners from the roaring '20s. A quintessential symphony of sound reverberated around the room as a big band broke out into a collective swing. Champagne bottles popped as gentlemen strutted between tables donning top hats and canes, pulling chairs gracefully out from behind their spouses.

"You see now, Max. This is what your city can be. It's what it always has been. The only question is, will you do something to save it from itself? Will you dig deep down, beneath the sand, beneath the shallow hull of poker chips and strip clubs? Because if not you, then who?"

The mirage began to fade with each tick of the clock. Its pearl-encrusted pendulum transported them through episodes of Atlantic City's history in all its trials and triumphs, developments and collusions.

"A godmother, Max, is a ship's spiritual guide," she continued. "A watchful guardian, bringing good luck and protection to all who sail aboard her vessel."

"Then who's the godmother for *M.S. World One*?" Max asked, wiping his eyes for reassurance that he wasn't dreaming.

"That's exactly my point. She'd not been christened yet. That's why she can't be repaired."

"So, who should we nominate? Aren't you the godmother?"

"No, Max, I'm the figurehead, or *maidenhead,* if you will. That's different than a godmother."

"How so? Can't you be both?"

"A ship like this can't just have one godmother."

"Why not? All other ships do."

"Because this ship... this ship belongs to the world."

An antique harp began to play as Ms. America faded back into the clock. Her ghostly aura dissipated as a ray of sunlight burst through the atrium.

Christened? How does she expect me to do that? Max looked around cluelessly, patting his pockets for a tool, a token, heck, even a few poker chips would be a start! *How am I ever going to see Ella again if I can't fix this bloody ship?* He paused, struck with an illuminating idea that sent shivers down his spine. *This ship can't just have one Godmother because this ship belongs to...*

"The world! That's it! I need to bring the world back to Atlantic City!" he shouted to an empty rotunda of silverware.

Patting his last jacket pocket, the heavy outline of his pocket-watch vibrated a serendipitous pulse. Uncovering its blinking blue hues with a shaky palm, he wound the clock back to his Embarkation Day in Playground Pier.

Pacing forward with an outstretched arm, he clicked the watch into the base of the grandfather clock as if surrendering the Holy Grail back to its rightful owner, offering the only possession he had left to give—his time.

Magically, the ship began to repair itself piece by piece. Chairs realigned as tablecloths folded atop freshly built furniture. Glass reassembled and fixtures molded back into their original positions. To Max, it felt and looked as though *M.S. World One* finally returned to her former glory, ready to sail away toward Europe and eventually back home, to Atlantic City.

Bells rang and champagne smashed alongside the newly christened vessel as it sailed east out of Cartagena. Citizens cheered the departure in grand celebration as they ran skittishly around the town center, rotating the coffee hourglass once again to signal the end of the day's events.

"Where have you been, mate? I've been looking all over for you?" Henk threw Max a pair of binoculars for the sail away on the bow.

"Had a bit of an excursion." Max smirked, tossing Tio's locket up and down in his hand. "Must have been beyond your watch?"

"Very funny." Henk chuckled, guiding them up the stairs to the observation deck.

The view from above was different this time. No sweeping panoramas or grand balconies. It appeared as though the whole ship was reassembled to fit into a divided frame. Everything seemed to look, and feel, like half the size of its former self.

"I've grown to like this much better." Henk glided his hands over the mahogany railings. "It's faster, sleeker, and more sustainable." He glanced over his shoulder at the solar-powered engine stacks and hydrofoils.

"We could use a bit more innovation around here," Max agreed, impressed with the renovations. "Look! What's that? Up ahead!"

Max turned back around in a flash to witness a storm cloud sweeping the horizon line. Its stratus formation created a thin barrier of dust stretching as wide as the eye could see. As their ship approached, a green light illuminated shadows behind its veil.

"Okay, okay! Enough chit-chat." Captain Lex flung open the door to the bridge, assuming his position at the helm.

"Max! care to do the honors?" He pointed toward a throttle lever on the refurbished control panel.

Well, this is a first. The captain trusting me to do something? Max celebrated, walking over to the panel.

"Full steam ahead!"

Landscapes shifted as the horizon warped with the passing ship when it sailed through the barrier. The vast Atlantic Ocean no longer loomed in front of them, but the appearance of a teal lagoon bordered with concrete forts and red-shingled roofs, defining the port of Mindelo, Cape Verde.

"Welcome to Africa," the captain announced, dusting off his hands before stepping down from the helm. "Whoa! This is much faster." He applauded the engineers.

Where is everyone? Max exited the bridge to have a look around the promenade.

"Henk! What happened to the passengers?" Max was somewhat afraid to know the truth.

"They're with Price, in the other half," Henk clarified, following closely behind as they toured the rest of the interior. Lounges, reception areas, Atlantis Hall, and Roulette Stage... All had been split down the middle and welded back into place. It appeared to be a spitting image of its former self, yet infinitely more sustainable.

"When we crashed, on the ridge, we thought you didn't make it. I mean, we were able to get most of the passengers to safety, some choosing to fly home, others trekked further south. I-I thought you were with Ella." Henk shrugged, trying to hide his expression so as not to upset him any further.

"Well, here I am." Max stretched his arms out in sarcastic amusement. "Wait, did you say Price is in the other half?"

"Yeah. Price, Ella, Daveed, and most everyone else. Passengers and all," Henk recited, taking a roll count with his fingers.

"Okay, so what's the plan?" Max strategized, looping the promenade in frustration.

"Captain needs to make a few stops first." Henk started to jog alongside him as he tried to keep pace.

"Great!" Max clutched Tio's locket around his neck. "Well, how long is that going to take?" he vented, kicking a cargo locker.

At this rate, it will take another week before I can be reunited with Ella, if she is even safe on Price's ship. Who knows what could have happened to her by now?

"Listen, mate, I know we've been through a lot. You just need to be patient. Haven't you read that old children's fable? The one with that rabbit and the lizard?"

"You mean the tortoise and the hare?" Max corrected, teeming with rage at his Dutch companion's feeble attempt to comfort his anguish. "Don't even start with me, Henk. Everyone knows that the hare should've won, but the tortoise cheated!" he scoffed, agitated by the remark, yet unwilling to accept the true moral of the fable.

"Cheating only gets you so far, kid." Captain Lex emerged onto the promenade; his sluggish stride inched closer as he paced the teak deck for the thousandth time. Board by board, he hobbled toward them. "Let's not be rash."

Rash? Rash! There's a time to stop and smell the roses, but it's certainly not now.

"We've prepped the lifeboats, manned the hoses, and triple-checked the propellers, Captain." Henk straightened his posture as he approached, pinching Max to follow his lead.

"Very good. You're dismissed." The captain took a seat on a utility bench as Henk returned to the bridge.

Attempting to evade what was sure to be a lengthy lecture, Max tried to slip inside.

"Wait right there," the captain ordered, waving him down to sit beside him.

So close. I don't want to hear another...

"Look, Max, we've come too far for you to just rush into this." The captain stroked his beard as he conjured up a narrative. "I never told you this, or anyone for that matter, so listen up." He pressed his watch into the wall behind them, initiating a projection that animated as he spoke. "I let you stay that day, back in Atlantic City, when you came aboard our ship. Do you know why?" A flashback of the embarkation cycled through a scene of shadows in front of him.

"Well, you said my heart was in the right place," Max recalled.

"Yes, but there's more to it than that. I let you stay because you reminded me of someone. Someone who came aboard the same way you did, except many years before."

Oh, great, now he's going into another long-winded recollection. What are these called again? Senior moments?

"A long time ago, on our first visit to Atlantic City, a boy crossed the gangway from the pier. Just as you did. Bright-eyed, full of wonder and amazement for this magnificent vessel." He pointed to the cityscape and boardwalks appearing out of the projection. "He begged me not to cast him back ashore, saying something about the lack of opportunity and development, disgruntled with the ruins of prohibition and amusements of the 1950s. 'I need to learn how to build a city in the sand!' he pleaded, compelled to usher in a new era filled with spectacles and thrills! So, I pitied him. Sympathized with his destitution and let him stay. Heck! I even taught him everything I knew. He was my prized pupil."

"Why are you telling me all of this?" Max nudged him out of his recollection.

"Because it was the greatest mistake of my life." The captain cringed, gripping the side of the bench as projections of overrun casinos, pillaged community chests, and a wicked figure donning a top hat and cane emerged through the mirage. "He abused my knowledge. Squandered it. His dream of building a city in the sand turned into an uncontrollable lust to defend his castle from the sea."

"So, why did you let me stay? What makes me any different?" Max confronted him, ripping the captain's watch from the wall to halt the projections.

"You're not," the captain replied. "Which is why you can't rush into this."

I'm sick of your outdated advice! Stop telling me what to do! We need to stop Price! We're running out of time!" Max exploded, running down the promenade and up the stairs to his cabin, slamming the door with disdain.

MEDITERRANEAN MADNESS

"Behold! The Rock of Gibraltar!" Captain Lex belted from the helm over the PA system. "Gateway to the Mediterranean!"

The 1400-foot apex watched over them like a silent guardian, closely following their vessel as it sailed around the Iberian Peninsula. Along the horizon, wild monkeys toyed with unsuspecting travelers as they trekked closer toward the summit.

A knock at Max's door pulled him from his view.

"Feeling better now, Max?" Henk propped open the door in a friendly embrace.

"Yeah, just needed to clear my head."

"Good. Get ready, I heard Price crossed the border a few months ago. There's no knowing how much damage he's done already."

Wakes rocked the ship as it listed violently from side to side, pushing them toward the islands of Minorca and Majorca like a toddler's cradle caught in a whirlpool. The coastline of Spain swept past their port hole, carving their arrival as it ushered them deeper into the region.

"Brace yourselves!" the captain warned as a rogue wave crashed into the hull, nearly capsizing it as sextants and navigation officers slid across the bridge.

Regaining his footing to assess the scene, Max peered through a periscope to investigate the cause of the swell. "There! Nine o'clock, portside!"

Passing around the periscope to brief the engagement team, they previewed the looming threat.

"Look! Over there! Just off the coast of Barcelona." Max watched in horror as Price's ship pulled alongside the pier, polluting black smoke into the air as it emptied its bilge pumps into the harbor. *It looks worse than Tio's cargo clipper. What happened?* A rusted gangway let down onto the pier as hundreds of orange-coat passengers disembarked into the streets like a wrangled mob, snapping photos and raiding souvenir shops to commence the day's bargain hunt.

Sighting the Mediterranean landscape through the periscope's mythical lens, Max was able to study the damage left behind in the ports of Valencia and Malaga. A trail of destitution, colonization, and anarchy ravaged the cityscapes. Merchants left fending off an army of tourists in a relentless barter exchange of foreign currency and overwhelming demand. Cathedrals crumbled with the stampede of excursionists snapping endless photographs on worn balconies desperately trying to preserve the essence of their heritage. Mayors lined their pockets with multicolored bills in celebration as they marveled at their cities being burned to the ground.

Pivoting his gaze from the pillage of ruin engulfing southwest Spain, Max focused into the streets of La Rambla as the weight of their gangway finally decimated the pier onto Barceloneta Beach. *We have to stop this!*

Thousands of tourists flocked the streets approaching Gaudi's Cathedral, *La Sagrada Familia*. Their utter neglect and disrespect for the natives radiated with each scoop of gelato and branded t-shirt. *I can't tell what's worse, the air emissions or people pollution?* Unchecked by the local law enforcement and desensitized to the prevailing customs, the alien hoard ransacked every corner cafe and quaint bistro of all the delicacies and WIFI bandwidth they could absorb. Just when the city reached its breaking point, a horn sounded from the ship's smokestack as a red light illuminated the skyline, signaling a repatriation of the gluttonous swarm of passengers.

"Onward! To Venice!" Price's voice boomed over the intercom, inciting a riotous mob to smash windows and break into storefronts in their march back aboard in preparation for their final sail away.

"We need to do something!" Max shouted, holstering the periscope.

"Bring us alongside!" Henk affirmed, rushing over to the controls to initiate the docking procedures as Captain Lex steadied the wheel.

Waves shook the hull as it crashed into the pier. Climbing down the mooring lines onto the dock, Henk and Max ran downtown to help salvage goods from the burning storefronts and crumbling balconies of ransacked homes lining *La Rambla.*

"Watch out!" Max warned as the statue of Christopher Columbus collapsed, nearly burying Henk in the rubble. Crowds of Spaniards wept in the streets as they clung to the ruins of its former glory. Barcelona was lost. Fire engulfed the remanence of *La Sagrada Familia* as citizens desperately tried to extinguish the flames of chaos spreading through the streets.

Just beyond their gaze, above the smoke and flames, flag poles proudly displayed a red banner with the bold letter "P" atop every cathedral in the city, signaling a complete takeover and expansion of the infamous Price Empire.

We can't let this happen again. Max fumed as they hobbled back to the ship.

The sting of failure lingered through the silence on the bridge as they limped inside the control room.

"Lex to Venice. Lex to Venice." The captain opened an emergency frequency, unable to connect.

"Any ideas?" Max nurtured second-degree burns as he scanned a map for the right approach.

"We won't be able to catch them in time." Henk calculated with a sextant and nautical chart. "Can we get a direct channel to the mayor?" he suggested, toggling through their communication dials for an open line.

Devastated by their failure to save Barcelona, Max looped the observation deck to diffuse his anguish. *How could this happen? There has to be a better way.*

Suddenly, a raven circled overhead, patroling the scene before swooping down to land on a nearby railing.

"Cera! I need your guidance," Max pleaded.

Answering his wish, she transformed back into human form. Embracing him in her arms, she absorbed the overwhelming failure of their pursuit like a motherly empath. "You've come so far, Max, don't give up now."

"I don't know what to do! We won't make it in time to save Venice!" He broke down, sulking hopelessly in her arms.

"Toughen up! Have I taught you nothing?!" She shook him out of his depression. "The world has a way of looking out for itself," she professed, shouldering his weight. "Empires rise and fall with the cycle of history, repeating themselves throughout eras and regions, indifferent to kings or peasants. The soul of our planet maintains its own delicate balance of nature, and our place within it," she continued, gazing into the distance.

"What do you mean? Isn't that what we're trying to stop Price from disrupting?" Max cried.

"Greed and possession are vices that tempt us all. No one is immune from their disease. But we can choose to rise above them," she preached.

"But I can't confront him. It's too late! He'll never change!"

"Maybe it's not up to you?" She unveiled the conductor's baton from Antarctica and handed it to him like they were in the midst of a relay race. "I'll warn the people of Venice," she promised, transforming back into a raven and flying ahead over the horizon.

Elated by her guidance, Max rushed back into the control room to find the Captain and Henk locked in a heated argument.

"No, no, no, we can't pull alongside Starboard! Their cannons are too powerful; we'll be pushed into the jetties. Damn it! We're outmuscled." Captain Lex pounded his fist on the table in frustration.

"Venice is ready." Max strutted back into the room, wielding the baton overhead.

"What? How?" Henk roused, demanding an explanation.

"Trust me. We don't have much time." Max unrolled a harbor chart, beginning to trace a blockade. "Price will likely pull alongside here." He pointed to the main terminal. "But a blockade will cut him off here." He pointed to an inlet slightly west of the pier. "While he's distracted, we can dispatch a zodiac to float alongside his portside anchor long enough for me to climb aboard through the cargo hold."

"You're not going alone! Are you crazy? You'll be cast overboard!" Henk blurted out.

Ignoring the protest, Max continued, "We'll commence at daybreak. Before his officers have enough time to patrol the bridge."

"What's your angle?" Captain Lex asked, sensing a hidden agenda. "Everyone knows you can't reroute a ship that big with one person."

"Keep the zodiac close and prep the lifeboats for lowering." Max plotted the evacuation coordinates before leaving the bridge for one last loop around the observation deck, savoring the red twilight of sunset as it dropped behind the outline of the approaching Venetian harbor.

Dusk turned to dawn as they approached the port of Venice. The quiet stillness of daybreak cut through the morning mist like a sleeping Goliath, waiting to be provoked. Just as planned, *M.S. World One* pulled alongside the main terminal, floating within striking distance of the pier.

"Look! The Venetians!" Henk ran toward the starboard-side railing for a closer look.

Peering through the Captain's periscope, Max couldn't believe his eyes. "They're blocking the harbor!" One by one, an armada of gondolas assembled an impenetrable barrier, prepared to protect their city from Price's arrival with their last dying breaths.

"Now, Henk! Bring us alongside!" Seizing the opportunity as a distraction, Captain Lex positioned them within distance of boarding, lowering the lifeboats and zodiac on cue as Max donned a lifejacket to grapple aboard.

"This is a one-way ticket," the captain warned, arming him with a hook and emergency flare. "Godspeed, Max." He bid farewell, saluting the heroic attempt.

Slicing relentlessly through the shallow tide, Henk propelled a zodiac in pursuit of the aft cargo bay. Idling alongside, Max loaded the grappling gun, attached the mooring lines, and climbed aboard.

Darkness consumed the maintenance shaft as Max slipped farther inside the steel hull, stealthily creeping toward a provisions locker beneath Atlantis Hall. *If I could just make it to the crew quarters, maybe there're still survivors.*

A maze of windowless bunked cabins lined the steerage beneath the waterline, crowded with cookie-cutter doorways displaying the number and function of each inhabitant.

He tapped each of the doors, signaling his arrival like a submerged U-boat primed for deployment.

"Max! Max! Is that really you?" Daveed's voice echoed through the corridor.

Listening for his location, Max scanned the remaining cabins, honing-in on his voice as he checked the locks.

"Over here, this way." The voice grew louder, still muffled by the aluminum doors as Max uncovered his door.

Picking the lock with the back of the conductor's baton, Max swung open the entrance to find Daveed handcuffed to a desk, the bulging bags beneath his eyes telling the tale of a thousand inmates. Restless and demoralized, he began reciting the trail of destruction burning in Price's wake since the separation.

"It was terrible. Merciless! An imperial pursuit to consume everything in his path."

"I saw. First it was Malaga, then Valencia, and even Barcelona. I can't even imagine the horror decimating Portugal and Greece." Max cringed, removing his lifejacket.

"There's still hope, but not if you're spotted." Max picked the lock to his cuffs as Daveed rummaged through a bedside trunk. "Here, put this on!" Daveed handed him an old officer's uniform, its bright orange stitching shouldering three golden stripes.

"Perfect. I look like a proper jacka—"

"—mariner. A proper Mariner," Daveed interjected, shuffling him out of the room. "Follow me through the corridor to the atrium, and please try to play the part? At least for a few moments. We can't afford any more slip-ups." He donned a spare set of stripes to avoid detection.

"But what about the rest of the crew?" Max fastened the last button on his jacket. "Where's Ella?"

"Price imprisoned them beneath Roulette Stage," Daveed explained as he led their marched up the corridor.

Hallways became obstacle courses as they narrowly evaded patrolling guards. Blending a crafty cadence of disguise with elusive steps, they finally approached the stage undetected.

"Pick the lock. I'll keep watch," Daveed whispered, shielding Max's stance in his shadow as he tinkered with the keyhole.

"Max! Is that you?" a familiar voice greeted them as they slipped inside. *So much for disguises.*

The room was lined with prison cells, each hosting the remaining members of the blue-coat resistance. Passengers, crew, and performers all shackled to the iron bars as they sat hopelessly glaring out of port holes at the Venetian skyline.

One by one, he set them free to gather around a circular table anchored in the center of the stage. Celebrating their reunion, the cohort embraced each other in heartfelt camaraderie after months of confinement.

Where's Ella? Max picked the last lock and searched every corner of the room. *She has to be here somewhere.*

"Okay, everyone! Listen up!" Daveed assembled them around the table, unraveling a map of the ship across its surface.

"We only have one shot at this, and we have to make it count." He borrowed the conductor's baton to outline his strategy. "Price is likely up in the Crow's Nest at the helm with the rest of his first officers." He pointed to the observation deck.

"That means we'll have to scale seven decks to reach him. Now each of those levels are patrolled by a surveillance unit with a direct line to the bridge. If anyone is detected, they'll be sure to sound the alarm and section off the water-tight doors, flooding each chamber to flush us out into the harbor."

Murmurs buzzed around the table as the militia weighed their odds of success.

"There's no other way," Daveed argued, tapping the map to seize back their attention.

"Yes, there is," Max interjected, pausing his search for Ella. "On my signal, I'll need you all to commandeer a lifeboat. Wait here for the crew alert alarm, then storm the promenade and release the hooks."

"What?" Daveed interrupted. "Isn't the plan to regain control of the ship? Not abandon it!"

"It's too late for that. We've done enough damage already." Max grabbed the baton back from him and headed toward the atrium alone.

Deck by deck, he scaled the levels to the Crow's Nest in disguise. Climbing past glaciers and jungles, cathedrals and beaches. Replaying each episode from the voyages of the past the higher he climbed, he saluted patrol officers in character as they checked his ID at every station.

"State your name and function," a curious guard demanded on the sixth deck.

"Safety Officer Maxwell."

"Maxwell? Weren't you rotated down to the engine room this season?"

"No, sir. That's Robert. Captain Price gave him a lashing for screwing up *fog watch*."

"Oh, right. Very well. Proceed."

Wiping the sweat from his forehead after the close encounter, Max finally reached the doorway to the Crow's Nest. Taking a deep breath, he kicked it in with one furious blow.

"Price! Your empire ends now!" He startled the command of officers manning the bridge.

"Ah, he rises from the depths yet again. There's just no getting rid of you, is there, Max?" Price mocked, gripping the helm in preparation to ram the blockade.

"Not just me, us," Max challenged, pointing out at the gondolas defending the pier.

"You really think a militia of riverboats can withstand thousands of pounds of steel?" Price laughed.

"You're not welcome here! Can't you see it? Leave! Now!"

"Max, Max, Max, we're not all that different, you and I." Price waved him toward the helm. "Look at you! You fill in that suit nicely now, don't you?" He pointed toward the stripes sewn to his shoulders.

"I'll never be like you," Max said in defiance, standing up to him. "All you feel is greed. The lust to control, to own, to capture everything in your path." He swayed, highlighting a board-game stationed in the center of a long conference table anchored beside the helm. Its overdeveloped houses and hotels marked each of the ports conquered since their division along the equator.

"Look at what you've destroyed! Generations of culture, washed away with one sweeping raid. How could you do this? The beauty? The harmony? The Republic? Why do you fear everything you can't control? The purity of that which you cannot buy?" He reached toward the armada with outstretched arms, trying desperately to plead with Price to change his mind.

"Ha! Such a naïve boy. This is the way it has always been, and always will be, and there's nothing you or anyone in your generation can do about it," Price lectured, ordering his guards to detain him. "Extend the plank! Here's another one for the sharks."

Clouds converged around the port as lightning struck the bow of *M.S. World One*, cracking the teak decks wrapping the promenade below a thirty-foot steel board protruding from the panoramic windows lining the Crow's Nest. Dragging Max's flailing body to the pinnacle of the plank, Price's henchmen disarmed him of his pocket-watch before casting it overboard into the water below.

"Oh, how could I forget?" Price waved a henchman to unveil a glass platform at the apex of the room. Its clear barrier resembled a fish tank as it imprisoned the silhouette of a woman handcuffed to a pole. "Such a talented girl."

A pair of officers dragged her out of the tube to cast her onto the plank, removing a Venetian mask shielding her face.

"Ella!" Max shouted, balancing over to her as they embraced above the waterline.

"I'm sorry, Max. You shouldn't have come here." She clung to him in tears, saving her footing from a near-fatal fall. "It's too late, he's already captured most of the Mediterranean. We failed."

Turning to gaze upon the beauty of the Venetian skyline one last time, he held her in a tight embrace, preparing to jump.

"Caw!" a raven flew past their perch, landing on the emergency alarm to signal one long blast from the bridge.

Suddenly, the thunder of revolution overwhelmed the promenade. Blue-coated resistance emerged from the bowels of the ship and stormed the lifeboats. Inspired by Max's speech, some orange-coat officers turned on Price, relinquishing their command and discarding their stripes overboard as they created a diversion.

"Follow me!" Ella led Max off the plank and away from the ledge as they ran back inside the Crow's Nest and down the marble staircase to the control room. An accordion of switches, buttons, and levers flashed in a rhythmic kaleidoscope in front of them. Still wielding the conductor's baton, Max smashed the kiosk, triggering the water-tight doors to open and ignite the auxiliary engines, creating an explosion in the stern as water rushed inside the hull.

"We don't have much time. Get to the lifeboats!" Ella shouted, racing out of the room and onto the promenade. Dazed and disoriented from the sparks shooting out of the control panel, Max stumbled after her.

"This way! One at a time, don't overload the bow!" Daveed directed passengers into their lifeboats as the ship began to sink.

"S.O.S.," Henk repeated on the radio intercom. "Max. Paging Max. Do you copy?"

"Yes! I'm here. Lifeboat 66. What's your position?"

"Never mind that. Look! The blockade!"

Swarms of gondolas reinforced the piercing hull of *M.S. World One*, pushing back with all their might as merchants and citizens flooded the docks, joining forces to fight back the advance. Inch by inch, they shoved the mighty steel prison away from the pier, dispatching tugboats and fishing clippers to aid in the rebellion as the ship began to list dangerously close to capsizing.

"Heave!" the crowd rallied, cheering in celebration as they finally broke the tipping point. Glass shattered hundreds of balconies as the roar of propellers breached the surface, sending Price and his empire into a fast descent to the bottom of the harbor.

The booming blare of a foghorn echoed from the bridge of their rescue clipper as Captain Lex maneuvered toward the conflict, triggering 196 lifeboats to scatter to safety in all directions before *M.S. World One's* final submersion. Crew members loaded into a fleet of buoyant transports representing every country in the world as they floated away from the scene, setting a repatriation course home.

Overwhelmed by the conflict, Max fainted onto the controls of Lifeboat 66, sending it on a return journey of its own.

BOARDWALK REPUBLIC

———

Vanishing prints of a runner's stride faded to dust in the sand as the sound of deep, rhythmic breathing echoed through the wind along the coast. His leisurely pace in harmony with the gentle sways of summer gusts, he strode past the demolition of fallen resorts, vibrant neighborhoods, and freshly dredged beaches. Waves swirled around nurturing pilings, jetting out from a sustainable pier as sand brushed against a welcome sign revealing the vision of a new glistening oasis.

Atlantic City: A Porthole to the World.

Clouds began to retreat, fading ominous shadows concealing newly restored marquis, illuminating the promise of an era crafted with virtue and bliss. A boardwalk married the coast. Built for parades of prominence, the christened wood now cushioned an approaching thunder of footsteps. Upon reaching the end, Max paused for a moment to rest, kicking and uncorking a glass bottle in the sand to unravel a message hidden within.

Meet me where our days begin and end, over the
line where time stops ticking.

Flipping the parchment over, he uncapped a calligraphy pen and replied:

Waves crash onto welcoming shores, flowing
across a pond of paradise we once adored.
Republics rise as Empires fall to usher in a new
era of life once and for all.

Magically, the message began to finish itself, as if written by the hand of a guardian angel:

There's so much I'm going to miss, especially your
tender kiss.
But always remember, it's not goodbye, it's sea
you soon!
I'll think of you when looking at the stars and
the moon.

Max shed a tear as he rolled the parchment back into the bottle and cast it back into the gulf stream, hoping it would one day find its way back along these radiant shores.

Turning to wipe the sand from his feet on the boardwalk, he caught a glimpse of himself in the glass entrance to the Ocean Resort. Much to his surprise, staring back at him was the silhouette of an old man. Donning a pin-striped suit, top hat, and cane, the weight of a lifetime of community service showed in every wrinkle on his forehead and bag under his eyes.

Mystically, his face transformed to reflect Max's expression. Dazed in an eternal state of reverie, he glanced back at himself in the old man's clothes. Twirling a cane as he extinguished a cigarette, he removed his top hat and monocle as if the great curse plaguing this city had finally been lifted.

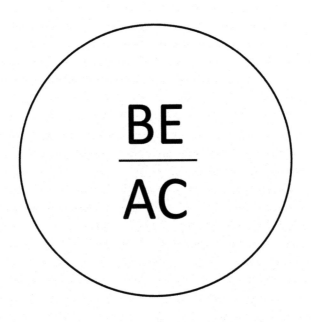

"**BE** a new era, we are **A**tlantic **C**ity."

End

ACKNOWLEDGMENTS

———

Boardwalk Republic couldn't have manifested without the inspiration and support of the following team of people:

- Eric Koester and the Creator's Institute for early coaching

- Holland America Line for inviting an opportunity to travel the world aboard a fleet of multinational cruise ships

- Brett Schiller for his mentorship, collaboration, and character contributions

- Tony Troy for his illustrations and visual storytelling

- The Schoedler Family for their encouragement, love, and support

- Our Beta Readers for their vital early feedback

- New Degree Press for endorsing and circulating the publication to national and international audiences

- University College London (UCL) for offering a safe-haven to international students during the COVID-19 pandemic

- Scholarship America for creating a young seafarer scholarship program

- Ocean City School District for their commitment to the future of South Jersey and sustainable community development

- Georgetown University for their commitment to alternative forms of education and hybrid learning

- Friends, Mentors, Coaches, and Diplomats for their years of service to their communities and countries

- Our presale contributors for early funding: Cindy Swenk, Ryan Heckler, Bruce Fischler, Barbara Daniel, Andrew DeMaria, and Chandre Anthony